S0-DUU-439

Collecting
The Tin Toy Car
1950-1970

by Dale Kelley

Schiffer Publishing Ltd

Box E, Exton, Pennsylvania 19341

Cover design and back cover design: Frank Held
Rex Barrett Collection
Copyright 1984 © by Dale Kelley.
Library of Congress Catalog Number: 84—51183

All rights reserved. No part of this work may be reproduced or used in any forms or by any means—graphic, electronic or mechanical, including photocopying or information storage and retrieval systems—without written permission from the copyright holder.

Printed in the United States of America.
ISBN: 0-88740-012-4
Published by Schiffer Publishing Limited, Box E, Exton, Pennsylvania 19341

First edition published in Great Britain and Europe
by New Cavendish Books—1984
23 Craven Hill, London W2 3EN
ISBN: 0-904568-30-50

This book may be purchased from the publisher.
Please include $1.50 postage.
Try your bookstore first.

ii

Table of Contents

Jason and Christopher Kelley

Dedication

To the new generation of toy collectors

The Author

Dale Kelley is the internationally known publisher of ANTIQUE TOY WORLD Magazine. Over the last twenty-five years he has devoted his life to the study of antique and contemporary toys. As a collector, he has amassed one of the great collections of post war tin cars in the world. Dale also enjoys collecting other types of toys from 1870 to the present. During his travels here and abroad, he has noted various changes in toy collecting that have evolved in recent years. Today's toy collector is seeking out toys made after World War II in greater numbers than ever before, with automotive toys taking the lead as one of the more popular choices among collectors.

In Dale's new book, "Collecting The Tin Toy Car: 1950-1970", the author has sought and received assistance from several prominent collectors in the United States and Europe. The book contains over 500 photographs, ranking it as one of the most comprehensive works of its kind. For the first time, the collector will be able to view and identify over 300 Post War toys with the aid of large color and black and white photos depicting many of the finest tin cars from this era. Dale not only features his impressive collection but also reveals rare examples of Post War tin cars from distinguished collections around the world. The author wishes to thank his many compatriots who shared their treasures for the enlightenment of us all.

Acknowledgments

This book would be lacking some of the most illustrious examples of post war tin toy cars if not for the help of my many collector friends at home and abroad. My heartfelt thanks to all of you. I would especially like to thank Rex Barrett, not only for photos but also for his technical expertise and loan of toys; and to Al Marwick, special thanks and appreciation for his journalistic capabilities.

Rex Barrett
Alexander Belevich
Jacky Broutin - Anamorphose
Jerry Byrne
Bill Drake
Gary Fox
C.W. Frey
Jack Herbert
Ron Hill
Ken Hutchinson
Dr. Reinhard Kunz
Don Lewis
Al Marwick
David Pressland
Jack Regan
Ron Smith
Fred Thompson

Foreword

For some twenty-five years following World War II the Japanese manufactured and distributed worldwide—attractive toy products.

They were made of tin with the automotive theme predominating.

In proportion to their participation the same held true for Western Germany. Great Britain and the United States, along with a few other countries, also contributed but the acclaim in the field belonged to the Japanese.

The medium is the collectible hand toy.

Roughly the items herein peaked in the 1950s, tapered off somewhat in the 1960s and then came to a virtual halt in the early '70s. The reason for their demise was rising labor rates and resulting inflation.

Little did the manufacturers of these Japanese and German toys realize that they were not only meeting a market for a child's plaything but that some day certain of their products would become poignantly involved in the adult psychology of collecting, of finding and possessing.

The psychology mentioned is intertwined with the artform of auto design in both replica and fantasy. They were intended, after all, to be just toys and not models hand sculptured in the studio of an auto manufacturer.

What determines, then, what toys become most collectible? Any miniature has ownership desire if it has identification for an individual. Craftsmanship, detail, product image, size of the toy, are all ingredients that bring a specimen to the forefront. In addition, rarity is always a factor.

The closer the toy is to replica the easier becomes its recognition. In defense of fantasy design, which certainly belongs, portrayal of the artform provides characterization and humor and stimulation the child can respond to.

We most likely will never again see the tin toy car as we knew it in the third quarter of the 20th Century. As our world society proceeds to refine itself the element of safety becomes a constant vigilance. Tin toys couldn't avoid some sharp edges.

With this practical and sensible thinking another golden era is in the past. But not without a certain sadness for the child who experienced these toy cars of tin.

What is left is the adult collector pursuing the toy he once owned, or the miniature of the car he once drove to his high school prom.

What has evolved is a boom in the 1980s in the collecting of vehicular toys. The category dominates and probably always will.

There is no association between man and material object like that existing between John Doe and his automobile. Or Mary Doe and hers. Contemporarily, it often reflects itself as a model or a toy or the collecting of same.

Dale Kelley has put together a photographic reference that will both serve and enthuse the hobby for years to come.

This book's segment in time is standing still—its pages waiting to be savored—on the shelf of a proud owner. The volume's owner will be even prouder if he or she has one or many of the examples illustrated. If not, the pictures become a tool in the search.

A fleet of tin toys somehow looms realistic and full size as its steward views and admires and ponders it.

Alone in secret moments.

---Al Marwick
"the fun is in the search"

5

A typical tin toy factory during the 1930's

Collecting The Tin Toy Car 1950-1970

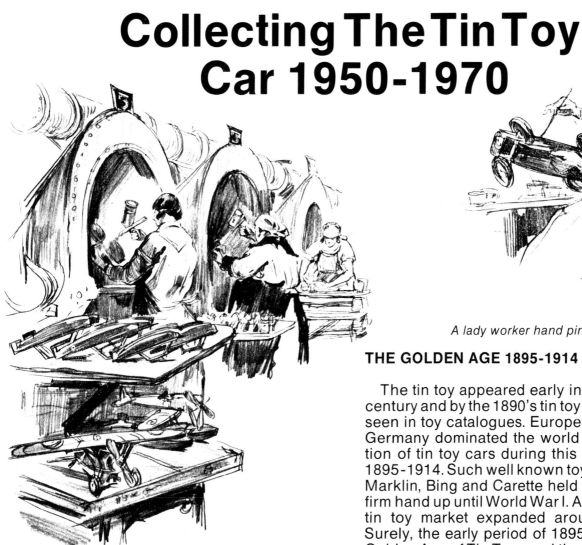

A lady worker hand pin-striping a tin car.

A tin toy factory dating from the 1930's. Workers are spray painting tin toys.

THE GOLDEN AGE 1895-1914

The tin toy appeared early in the nineteenth century and by the 1890's tin toy cars were to be seen in toy catalogues. Europe and especially Germany dominated the world in the production of tin toy cars during this early period of 1895-1914. Such well known toy companies as Marklin, Bing and Carette held the market in a firm hand up until World War I. After the war, the tin toy market expanded around the world. Surely, the early period of 1895-1914 was the Golden Age of Tin Toys and the most elaborate tin autos were made in this period, not to mention the other remarkable tin ships, trains, and novelty items.

Mass Production 1918-1939

During the period between 1918 to 1939, toy companies around the world would mass produce thousands of tin toy cars. Germany would still dominate the market with over a dozen toy companies producing tin-plate toy autos and trucks. But England, France, Spain, Italy, Japan and the United States were cutting into the market.

After World War II, a few of the bigger toy companies in Europe would start production once again. Schuco, Arnold, Joustra, Distler, Gama, Guntherman, J.N.F., Tipp and Co. were all producing some great tin cars during the 1950's and 1960's, but one by one they would all fall under to the keen competition of the ever growing Japanese toy Industry. The remaining few toy companies in Germany that lasted into the 1970's were producing toy cars in plastic.

Toy cars were made in many different materials over the last one hundred years; cast iron, steel, tin, wood, paper, glass, celluloid, plastic, rubber, die cast, etc. This book deals with toy cars made between 1950-1970 of tin-plate. The tin came in large pressed sheets from 8 ml. to 30 ml. thick. Most of the cars pictured in this book are 10 ml. thick, or for example, the thickness of a tin can. The large sheets of tin-plate first were lithographed with special presses and then cut-out and formed into various parts for tin toys. Although many of these tin toys were lithographed, some of them were spray painted and finished by hand. In the early years of tin toy manufacturing many of the tin toys were held together by solder or tab and slot. Most of the tins toys after World War II were still held together by tab and slot but screws were being used in some cases.

The Last of The Great Tin Toy Cars 1950-1970

The last of the great tin toy cars were produced mostly by toy companies of Japan with such strange sounding names as Bandai, Marusan, Alps, Asahi, Yonezawa and Haji, to name a few. In all, thirty toy companies are represented by the more than three hundred Japanese tin cars that we have pictured in this book.

Little is known about the post War Japanese toy industry. The toy companies of Europe and the United States before World War II are well-documented and much has been learned in the last ten years about the history of these great toy firms. We are just beginning to explore the complexity of the great toy industry of post War Japan. In the years to come, as the hobby of collecting Japanese toys gains in popularity, more research will most likely follow by toy collectors around the world. They will unearth new toy discoveries and learn more about the companies that produced these great toys.

We do know that Japan's toy industry started up around 1947 after World War II and expanded to three-hundred factories producing toys or parts for toys, mostly concentrated in the Eastern part of Tokyo (Koto District). A few of the toy factories were located in Osaka.

These toy factories were converted from military factories thus enabling the use of much of the War machinery in the production of tin toys. Most of the Japanese toy factories would form a pyramid system. Whereas making the main part themselves and subcontracting the remaining parts to piece-work factories located near by, they were able to expand the toy industry much faster. By 1962 the Japanese were exporting 83 million dollars in toys a year. Fifty-five percent of these toys were exported to the United States alone and the rest were sent around the world.

During the 1950s and 1960s the Japanese toy makers achieved a realism in the tin toy car never before seen. A 1956 Ford looked just like the real car. Many of the toy cars and trucks pictured in this book are exact replicas. This is one of the main reasons for their high collectibility at the present.

But like their counterparts before the War, the great tin toy industry of Japan would fall and by the early 1970s some of the larger toy companies like Bandai would be producing their extensive line of toy cars also in plastic and little by little would succumb to countries with cheap labor like Korea and Hong Kong.

Today, tin toys are still being produced in countries like China, Mexico and some of the third world countries but we will never see again the quality or quanity of the great tin toy as was produced by the great toy firms throughout history for the last one hundred and fifty years. Today, collectors in all parts of the world are seeking out these great tin treasures to protect and share with generations to come. All the toy cars pictured in this book are from the collection of Dale Kelley unless otherwise noted.

The above photos illustrate the process in making a Tin Toy car. Tin sheets are lithographed, then cut and formed into various parts. Notice, the finished toy car to the right. (Photograph courtesy Les Jouets 1909)

Japan's Toy Industry

In the above photo, you will note the trade mark on the back end of the race car (E.T. Co.). The other side of the race car has the trade mark (Y) inside a clover leaf and on the box the trade mark (Y) again. All three trade marks are pictured below. We know that (Y) stands for the Yonezawa Toy Co., but the (E.T. Co.) is still a mystery. Why the two different trade marks on the same toy? In the next few years as more research goes into the Japanese Toy Industry, many of these mysteries will be solved. Page 9 illustrates forty trade marks from the post war Japanese Toy industry. Most of them are well known toy companies or distributers. We will not discuss the European Toy Industry at this time because it is well documented and illustrated in many toy books already.

Japanese Toy Companies Trade Marks

1. Asahi Toy Co. Ltd. (A.T.C.)
2. Bandai (B)
3. Masudaya Toy Co. (TM)
4. Nomura Toy Ltd. (T.N.)
5. Unknown
6. Yonezawa (Y)
7. Unknown (M)
8. Asakusa Toys (A1)
9. Nemoto
10. Suda (SK)
11. Kosuge (KO)
12. Ahi
13. Alps
14. Cragstan (Distributer)
15. S.S.S. (Distributer)
16. Marusan (SAN)
17. Unknown
18. Unknown (MSK)
19. Rock Valley Toys
20. Tomy
21. Line Mar Toys
22. Marusan (SAN)
23. Daiya
24. Daishin Kogyo (DSK)
25. Unknown (KTS)
26. Kanto Toys
27. Taiyo Toys
28. Unknown (SH)
29. Ichida
30. Usagiya
31. Unknown (MKK)
32. Unknown (SY)
33. Taiyo Toys
34. Toy Nomura (T.N.)
35. Haji
36. To Play Ltd. (T.P.S.)
37. Kiyoshi Toys
38. Yamaichi
39. Ichiko
40. I.Y. Metal Toys

JAMES BOND
SPECIAL AGENT 007
ASTON MARTIN DB 5

GAMA-Spielzeug-formschön-preiswert-stabil-GAMA-Spielzeug

bekannt aus
den Filmen
GOLDFINGER
und
FEUERBALL

formschön
preiswert
stabil

JAMES BOND
007

	No. 4900		No. 4907	
	Originalmodell	Original model	Modèle original	
			4,5 V-Elektromotor	○
			4,5 V electric motor	
			moteur électrique (4,5 V)	
			elektrische Fernbedienung - Funktions-auslösung vom Batteriehalter aus	○
			electric remote control effected from a battery-box	
			les différentes fonctions s'effectuant par téléguidage électrique	
			Automatisches Wendewerk	○
			Mystery action	
			Système non stop	
○			Patentlaufzielwerk	
			Patent clockwork	
○			Moteur à ressort breveté	
			Mit Hand lenkbar	
○			steerable by hand	
			roues orientables	
			Mechanisch-automatisches Funktionssystem	
○			Mechanical-automatical system	
			Fonctionnement mécanique et automatique	
			2 ausfahrbare Maschinengewehre mit elektrischem Mündungsfeuer	○
○			2 hidden machine guns, red fire at gun muzzle	
			2 mitrailleuses escamotables avec flammes	
○			Schußgeräusch	shooting noise	bruit de tir	○
			ausfahrbare Rammhörner	
○			crash bumpers which can be extended and retracted	○
			pare-chocs télescopiques	
			Katapultsitz	
○			Ejector seat	○
			dispositif de catapultage avec siège éjectable	
			Versenkbarer Kugelfang	
○			Bullet proof shield goes up and down	○
			Pare-balles escamotable	
			Wechselbares Nummernschild	
○			License plates revolve	
			Plaque minéralogique interchangeable	

VERKAUFSLIZENZ FÜR WESTEUROPA (AUSSER ENGLAND)
SALES LICENSE FOR WESTERN EUROPE (ENGLAND EXCEPTED)
LICENCE DE VENTE POUR L'EUROPE OCC., A L'EXCEPTION DE L'ANGLETERRE

#1
Aston-Martin DB5 (James Bond)
Color: Grey
Length: 11 1/2"
MFG.: Gilbert, Japan
Year: 1960s

Note: See Gama Toy Catalog. The German Toy Co. (Gama) also made the James Bond Aston Martin.

#3A
Aston-Martin DB6
Color: Red
Length: 11"
MFG.: (A.T.C.) Asahi Toy Co., Japan
Power: Friction
Year: 1965

David Pressland Collection

#2
Aston Martin (James Bond)
Color: Gold
Length: 12"
MFG.: Gilbert, Japan
Power: Battery
Year: 1960s

Jerry Byrne Collection

#3
Aston Martin DB6
Color: Red
Length: 11"
MFG.: (A.T.C.) Asahi Toy Co., Japan
Year: 1960s

Ron Smith Collection

#4
Buick
Color: Grey also red and yellow
Length: 11"
MFG.: (T.N.) Toy Nomura
Power: Friction
Year: 1959

Note: Also came with battery powered motor.

#5
Buick LeSabre
Color: Blue
Length: 19"
MFG.: (ATC) Asahi Toy Co., Japan
Power: Friction
Year: 1966

#6
Buick
Color: Red
Length: 16"
MFG.: (T.N.) Toy Nomura
Power: Friction
Year: 1961

#7
Buick Emergency Car
Color: White
Length: 14"
MFG.: (T.N.) Toy Nomura
Power: Friction
Year: 1961

Jerry Byrne Collection

#8
Buick
Color: Blue
Length: 15"
MFG.: Ichiko
Power: Friction
Year: 1964

Ron Smith Collection

#9
Buick Wildcat
Color: Tan
Length: 15"
MFG.: Ichiko
Power: Friction
Year: 1963

Jerry Byrne Collection

#10
Buick Sportswagon
Color: White
Length: 15"
MFG.: Asakusa
Power: Friction
Year: 1968

Jerry Byrne Collection

#11
Buick
Color: White and blue
Length: 12"
MFG.: Ichiko
Power: Friction
Year: 1959

David Pressland Collection

#12
Buick
Color: Brown and white
Length: 17 1/2"
MFG.: Ichiko
Power: Friction
Year: 1960

David Pressland Collection

#16
Buick
Color: Grey and black
Length: 7"
MFG.: Marusan
Power: Friction
Year: 1953

Note: On the cover of the box, the statement "Sister car of our famous 'Cadillac'". Referring to the Marusan '51 Caddy.

#17
Futuristic Buick
Color: Black
Length: 7 1/2"
MFG.: Yonezawa
Power: Friction
Year: 1951

Ron Smith Collection

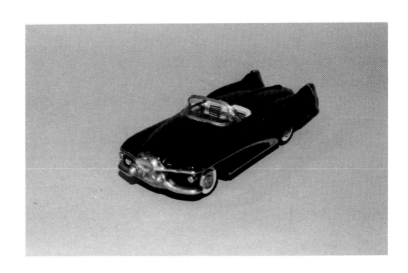

#18
Cadillac
Color: Creme body, green roof
Length: 11"
MFG.: Marusan
Power: Battery (Electric lights)
Year: 1951

Note: The Marusan Cadillacs with electric motor and lights are very rare.

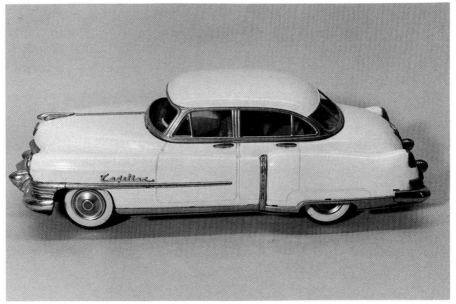

#19
Cadillac
Color: Gold
Length: 11"
MFG.: Marusan
Power: Battery (Electric lights)
Year: 1951

Note: This gold color Caddy by Marusan is very rare.

#20
Cadillac
Color: Grey, white, black red (only known colors).
Length: 11"
MFG.: Marusan
Power: Friction
Year: 1951

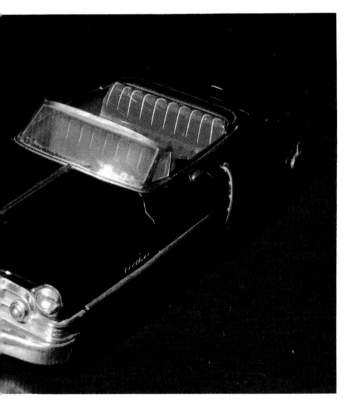

#21
Cadillac
Color: Known colors are grey, black, red, maroon, green, and blue.
Length: 11 1/2"
MFG.: Alps
Power: Friction
Year: 1952

Note: All Cadillacs from the Bill Drake Collection except for the grey Cadillac.
Original box - Rex Barrett Collection

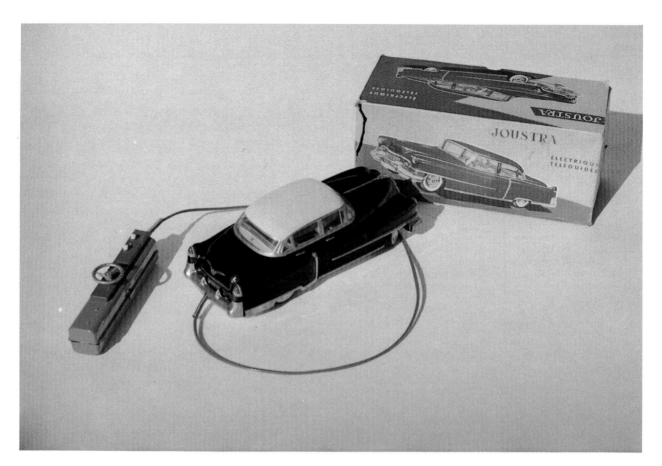

#22
Cadillac
Color: White and black
Length: 12"
MFG.: Joustra
Power: Battery
Year: 1954

Fred Thompson Collection
Ron Hill Collection
Note: Marusan from Japan was the first to produce this Cadillac, then the Gama Toy Co. from Germany. Joustra from France was the last toy company to use the dies. Sometimes you will see the Gama trademark on the Joustra Cadillac.

#23
Cadillac
Color: Black
Length: 13"
MFG.: (T.N.) Toys Nomura
Power: Battery (Elec. Lights)
Year: 1952

#24
Cadillac
Color: Red
Length: 11"
MFG.: Bandai
Power: Friction
Year: 1959

#25
Cadillac
Color: White
Length: 11"
MFG.: Bandai
Power: Friction
Year: 1959

#26
Cadillac
Color: Copper
Length: 11"
MFG.: Bandai
Power: Friction Year: 1960

Note: Original box

#27
Cadillac
Color: Black
Length: 11"
MFG.: Bandai
Power: Friction
Year: 1960

#28
Cadillac
Color: Black with white trim
Length: 18"
MFG.: (Y) Yonezawa
Power: Friction
Year: 1960

#29
Cadillac
Color: Red
Length: 22"
MFG.: (Y) Yonezawa
Power: Friction
Year: 1962

#30
Cadillac
Color: Creme
Length: 17 1/2"
MFG.: SSS
Power: Friction
Year: 1961 Fleetwood

#31
Cadillac
Color: Red
Length: 10 1/2"
MFG.: K.O.
Power: Friction
Year: 1967

Ron Smith Collection

#32
Cadillac
Color: Red and white
Length: 22"
MFG.: Ichiko
Power: Friction
Year: 1965

Ron Smith Collection

#33
Cadillac
Color: White
Length: 17"
MFG.: Bandai
Power: Friction
Year: 1963

Note: Box cover illustrates a '61 Caddy.

#34
Cadillac
Color: Gold
Length: 17"
MFG.: Bandai
Power: Friction
Year: 1960's

Jerry Byrne Collection

#35
Cadillac El Dorado
Color: Blue
Length: 10 3/4"
MFG.: Unknown, Japan
Power: Friction
Year: 1967

Jerry Byrne Collection

#36
Cadillac
Color: Blue
Length: 13"
MFG.: Bandai
Power: Battery
Year: 1969

Jerry Byrne Collection

#37
Cadillac
Color: Red
Length: 28"
MFG.: Ichiko
Power: Friction
Year: 1967

#38
Cadillac
Color: Red
Length: 17"
MFG.: (A.T.C.) Asahi Toy Co., Japan
Power: Friction
Year: 1965

#39 (Pages 30-31)
Chevrolet
Color: Grey-Black
Length: 11"
MFG.: Marusan Co. Ltd. Trademark (SAM)
Power: Friction motor
Year: 1954

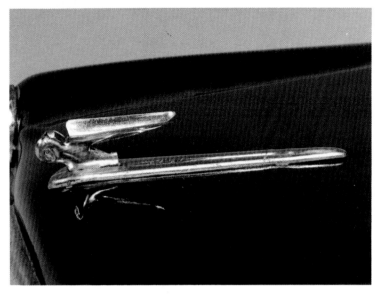

Packard

Mercedes

Chevrolet

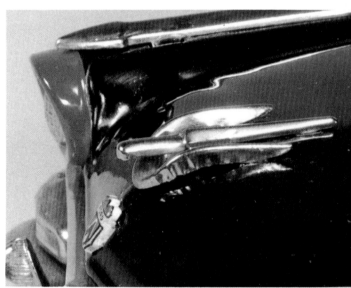

Ford

Edsel

Cadillac

#40
Chevrolet
Color: Black and white
Length: 10 3/4''
MFG.: Marusan
Power: Battery (Electric headlights)
Year: 1955

Ron Hill Collection

#41
Chevrolet
Color: Red
Length: 11 1/2''
MFG.: S.Y.
Power: Friction
Year: 1959

#42
Chevrolet
Color: Yellow
Length: 11"
MFG.: (A.T.C.) Asahi Toy Co.
Power: Friction
Year: 1962

#43
Chevrolet
Color: Blue
Length: 10 3/4"
MFG.: N K Toys, Korea
Power: Friction
Year: 1962

#44
Chevrolet Impala
Color: Blue and white
Length: 18"
MFG.: (T.N.) Toy Nomura
Power: Friction
Year: 1963

#45
Chevrolet
Color: Blue
Length: 14 1/2"
MFG.: Unknown
Power: Friction
Year: 1962

#46
Chevrolet Impala Convertible
Color: White
Length: 11"
MFG.: Bandai
Power: Friction
Year: 1961

#47
Chevrolet Impala Sedan
Color: Creme
Length: 11"
MFG.: Bandai
Power: Friction
Year: 1961

Note: Original box

#48
Chevrolet
Color: White and red
Length: 11"
MFG.: Marusan
Power: Friction
Year: 1960

#49
Corvair
Color: White
Length: 9"
MFG.: Unknown, Japan
Power: Friction
Year: 1963

#50
Chevrolet Corvette
Color: Red and silver
Length: 9 1/2"
MFG.: (Y) Yonezawa
Power: Friction
Year: 1958

#51
Chevrolet Corvette
Color: White and black
Length: 8"
MFG.: Bandai, Japan
Power: Battery
Year: 1962

#52
Chevrolet Corvette
Color: Red
Length: 8"
MFG.: Bandai
Power: Friction
Year: 1963

#53
Chevrolet Corvette
Color: Red
Length: 12 1/2"
MFG.: Ichida, Japan
Power: Battery
Year: 1964

#54
Chevrolet Corvette
Color: White
Length: 9 1/2"
MFG.: Taiyo, Japan
Power: Battery
Year: 1968

#55
Chevrolet Camaro
Color: White
Length: 11"
MFG.: Modern Toys
Power: Friction
Year: 1967

Jerry Byrne Collection

#56
Chevrolet Camaro
Color: Black and white
Length: 11"
MFG.: Modern Toys
Power: Friction
Year: 1967

Jerry Byrne Collection

#57
Chevrolet Camaro
Color: Red
Length: 14"
MFG.: (T.N.) Toy Nomura
Power: Friction
Year: 1967

#58
Chevrolet Camaro
Color: Red
Length: 9 1/2"
MFG.: Taiyo, Japan
Power: Friction
Year: 1967

#59
Chevrolet Camaro
Color: Red, white, and blue
Length: 9 1/2"
MFG.: Taiyo, Japan
Power: Battery
Year: 1971

#60
Corvair Bertone
Color: White
Length: 12"
MFG.: Bandai
Power: Battery
Year: 1963

#61
Chevrolet Corvair
Color: White and blue
Length: 9"
MFG.: Ichiko
Power: Friction
Year: 1963

Jerry Byrne Collection

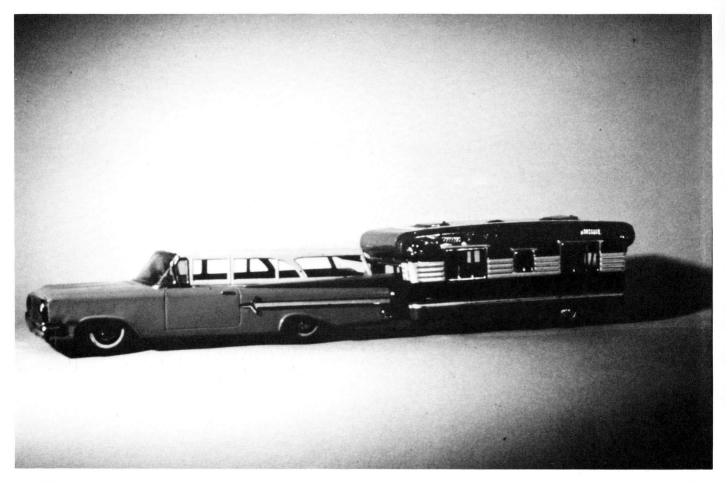

#62
Chevrolet Wagon
Color: Two tone blue
Length: 12"
MFG.: Unknown, Japan
Power:
Year: 1960

Trailer
Length: 9 1/2"
MFG.: SSS

David Pressland Collection

#63
Chevrolet Trailer
Color: White
Length: 8" - overall 16 1/2"
MFG.: Bandai
Power: Friction
Year: 1964

#64
Citroen
Color: Blue and white
Length: 12"
MFG.: Bandai, Japan
Power: Friction
Year: 1950 - 60's

Note: Bandai also made the Citroen in an eight inch model and the eleven inch model came both in a friction and battery version. (Red and white or blue and white).

#65
Citroen
Color: Red and white
Length: 8"
MFG.: Joustra, France
Power: Friction
Year: 1950's

セリカダブルエックス

CELICA
X
2000G

#66
Celica
Color: Red
Length: 14"
MFG.: Ichiko, Japan
Power: Friction
Year: 1979

#67
Berlina (Datsun)
Color: Red and white
Length: 10 1/2"
MFG.: Unknown, Japan
Power: Friction
Year: 1960's

#68
Datsun Nissan Gloria Hardtop GL
Color: Yellow and black
Length: 16"
MFG.: Ichiko, Japan
Power: Friction
Year: 1970's

#69
Datsun 2000 Fair Lady Z
Color: Red
Length: 18"
MFG.: Ichiko
Power: Friction
Year: 1970's

#70
Datsun Fair Lady Z
Color: Red
Length: 18"
MFG.: Ichiko, Japan
Power: Friction
Year: 1972

#71
Chrysler Imperial
Color: Blue
Length: 16"
MFG.: (A.T.C.) Asahi Toy Co.
Power: Friction
Year: 1962

Note: This Chrysler is very rare, ony a few are known in collections around the world.

#72
Chrysler Imperial
Color: Red
Length: 16"
MFG.: ATC
Power: Friction
Year: 1962

(Photo of original box - Rex Barrett Collection)
Note: Only red Chrysler known in a collection.
(Dr. Reinhard Kunz/Switzerland Collection and photo)

#73
Divco Dugan's Bakery Truck
Color: White and black
Length: 7 1/2"
MFG.: Unknown, Japan
Power: Friction
Year: 1950's

#74
Dodge
Color: Red and white
Length: 11"
MFG.: (T.N.) Toy Nomura
Power: Friction
Year: 1958

#75
Dodge Yellow Cab
Color: Yellow
Length: 12"
MFG.: (T.N.) Toy Nomura
Power: Friction
Year: 1968

#76
Dodge
Color: Green
Length: 24"
MFG.: (M) Japan
Power: Friction
Year: 1959

#77
Dodge
Color: Red and white
Length: 18 1/2"
MFG.: (M)
Power: Friction
Year: 1959

Note: The Japanese made few trucks. The Dodge pickup is one of the better examples. Note the size- 18 1/2" long. Original pull cords.

#78
Ferrari and Speed Boat
Color: White
Overall Length: 23".
MFG.: Bandai and Fleetline
Year: 1958

Note: Ferrari also sold by Bandai without boat (colors known: white and green)

#79
Ferrari
Color: Silver
Length: 11"
MFG.: Bandai, Japan
Power: Battery
Year: 1958

#80
Ferrari 250 G
Color: Red
Length: 9 1/2"
MFG.: (A.T.C.) Asahi Toy Co.
Power: Friction
Year: 1957

Jerry Byrne Collection

#81
Ford Flower Delivery Wagon
Color: Blue
Length: 12"
MFG.: Bandai
Power: Friction motor
Year: 1955

Note: These delivery wagons seem to be on the rare side.

#82
Ford Standard Fresh Coffee Wagon
Color: Black and orange
Length: 12"
MFG.: Bandai
Power: Friction motor
Year: 1955

Note: Very rare

#83
Ford Station Wagon
Colors: Creme and black, two tone green, red and black
Length: 12"
MFG.: Bandai
Power: Friction
Year: 1955

#83a
Ford Wagon
Length: 12"
Color: Black - Orange
MFG.: Unknown
Power: Friction
Year: 1960

Jack Herbert Collection

#84
Ford Ranchero
Color: Two tone blue
Length: 12"
MFG.: Bandai
Power: Friction
Year: 1955

Ron Smith Collection

61

#85
Ford
Color: Black, blue and red
Length: 12"
MFG.: (Y) Yonezawa
Power: Friction
Year: 1956

Rex Barrett Collection

#85a
Ford
Color: White - Blue
Length: 12"
MFG.: Ichiko
Year: 1957

Jack Herbert Collection

#86
Ford Good Humor Ice Cream Truck
Color: White
Length: 10 3/4"
MFG.: (KTS), Japan
Power: Friction motor
Year: 1950

#87
Ford Thunderbird
Colors: Red, red and black
Length: 8"
MFG.: Bandai
Power: Friction motor
Year: 1962

#88
Ford Thunderbird
Color: Red
Length: 11"
MFG.: (Y) Yonezawa
Power: Battery motor
Year: 1962

#89
Ford Thunderbird
Color: Red
Length: 12"
MFG.: (A.T.C.) Asahi Toy Co.
Power: Friction
Year: 1964

#90
Ford Thunderbird
Color: Red
Length: 11"
MFG.: Cragstan, Japan
Power: Battery
Year: 1962

#91
Ford Thunderbird
Color: Red and black
Length: 10 3/4"
MFG.: Bandai
Power: Friction
Year: 1965

#92
Ford Thunderbird
Color: Red
Length: 16"
MFG.: Ichiko
Power: Friction
Year: 1964

Ron Smith Collection

#93
Ford Thunderbird
Color: White
Length: 12 1/2"
MFG.: (A.T.C.) Asahi Toy Co.
Power: Friction
Year: 1964

Jerry Byrne Collection

#94
Ford Thunderbird
Color: Red
Length: 15 1/2"
MFG.: Unknown, Japan
Power: Friction
Year: 1964

Jerry Byrne Collection

#95
Ford Thunderbird
Color: White and red
Length: 11 1/4"
MFG.: Unknown, Japan
Power: Friction
Year: 1961

Jerry Byrne Collection

#96
Edsel Convertible
Color: Green
Length: 10 1/4"
MFG.: Haji
Power: Friction
Year: 1958

Al Marwick Collection

#97
Edsel Wagon
Color: Black and red
Length: 10 1/2"
MFG.: Haji
Power: Friction
Year: 1958

Al Marwick Collection

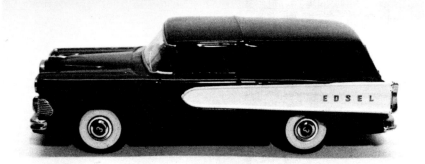

#98
Edsel Station Wagon
Color: Red, white and black
Length: 11"
MFG.: (T.N.), Japan
Power: Friction
Year: 1958

#98A
Ford Edsel
Color: White and orange
Length: 10 1/2"
MFG.: Yonezawa
Power: Friction
Year: 1960's

David Pressland Collection

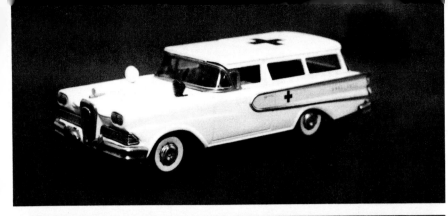

#99
Edsel Ambulance
Color: White
Length: 11"
MFG.: Haji
Power: Friction
Year: 1958

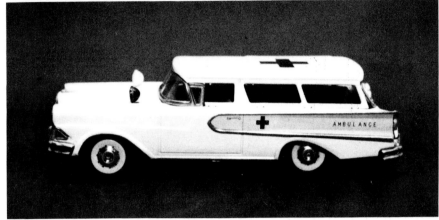

#100
Edsel
Color: Green and white
Length: 10 3/4"
MFG.: (A.T.C.) Asahi Toy Co.
Power: Friction
Year: 1958

#101
Edsel
Color: Blue and white
Length: 8 1/2"
MFG.: (T.N.) Toy Nomura
Power: Friction
Year: 1958

#102
Ford
Color: Green and white
Length: 11"
MFG.: Cragstan
Power: Battery
Year: 1958

#103
Ford
Color: Red and white
Length: 11"
MFG.: Unknown, Japan
Power: Friction
Year: 1959

#104
Ford
Color: Red and black
Length: 11"
MFG.: Unknown, Japan
Power: Friction
Year: 1960

#105
Ford Country Sedan
Color: Blue and white
Length: 10 1/2"
MFG.: Bandai, Japan
Power: Friction motor
Year: 1961

#106
Ford Galaxie
Color: Black and blue
Length: 11"
MFG.: Modern Toys
Power: Friction
Year: 1965

Jerry Byrne Collection

#107
Ford (Retractable top)
Color: Red and black
Length: 10"
MFG.: (K) Japan
Power: Friction
Year: 1958

Jerry Byrne Collection

#108
Ford Fairlane
Color: Red and white
Length: 10"
MFG.: Ichiko
Power: Friction
Year: 1957

Ron Smith Collection

#109
Ford
Color: White and blue
Length: 12"
MFG.: Unknown, Japan
Power: Friction
Year: 1959

Ron Smith Collection

#110
Ford Country Sedan
Color: Mint green and white
Length: 12"
MFG.: Asahi Toy Company (ATC)
Power: Friction
Year: 1962

Al Marwick Collection

#111
Ford
Color: Red and white
Length: 13"
Power: Friction
Year: 1964

Ron Smith Collection

#112
Ford
Color: Light brown
Length: 17"
MFG.: Rico, Spain
Power: Friction
Year: 1964

Ron Smith Collection

#113
Ford
Color: Blue
Length: 17"
MFG.: Rico, Spain
Power: Friction
Year: 1964

Ron Smith Collection

#114
1961 Asahi Toy Co., Ltd. (Japan)
Toy catalog A.T.C.
Anamorphose - Jacky Broutin
Collection.

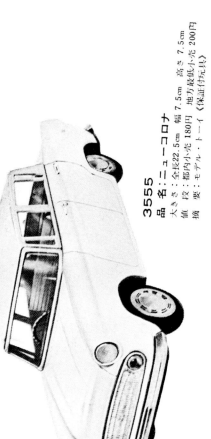

3555
品　名：ニューコロナ
大きさ：全長22.5cm　幅 7.5cm　高さ 7.5cm
値　段：都内小売 180円　地方最低小売 200円
摘　要：モデル・トーイ　《保証付玩具》

2999
品　名：フォード・エドセル
大きさ：全長28cm　幅12cm　高さ 8.5cm
値　段：都内小売 350円　地方最低小売 380円
摘　要：モデル・トーイ　《保証付玩具》

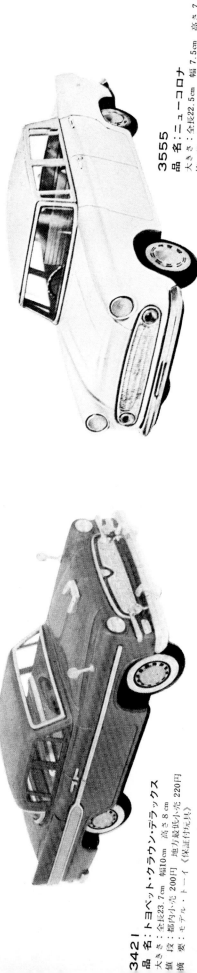

3557
品　名：ルノー・フロリード
大きさ：全長23.5cm　幅 9.5cm　高さ 7.5cm
値　段：都内小売 250円　地方最低小売 270円
摘　要：モデル・トーイ　《保証付玩具》最高の製品です

3421
品　名：トヨペット・クラウン・デラックス
大きさ：全長23.7cm　幅10cm　高さ 8 cm
値　段：都内小売 200円　地方最低小売 220円
摘　要：モデル・トーイ　《保証付玩具》

2791
品　名：10時フォード
大きさ：全長25cm　幅11cm　高さ 7.7cm
値　段：都内小売 250円　地方最低小売 270円
摘　要：モデル・トーイ　《保証付玩具》

#115
Ford Mustang
Color: Red
Length: 11"
MFG.: Bandai, Japan for Sears
Power: Battery
Year: 1965

#116
Ford Mustang (FBI)
Color: Black and white
Length: 11"
MFG.: Bandai
Power: Friction
Year: 1965

#117
Ford Mustang (Do it yourself kit)
Color: White
Length: 6 1/2"
MFG.: Haji
Power: Friction
Year: 1966

#118
Ford Mustang
Color: Red
Length: 14"
MFG.: Yonezawa, Japan
Power: Battery
Year: 1965

Note: Original box

#119
Ford Mustang
Color: Red
Length: 13"
MFG.: Bandai
Power: Battery
Year: 1967

#120
Ford Mustang
Color: Silver and black
Length: 11"
MFG.: Bandai
Power: Battery
Year: 1965

Note: Original box

#121
Ford Mustang
Color: Red
Length: 15 1/2"
MFG.: (T.N.) Toys Nomura
Power: Battery
Year: 1965

Jerry Byrne Collection

#122
Ford Mustang
Color: Blue
Length: 13 1/2"
MFG.: Yonezawa
Power: Battery
Year: 1965

#123
Ford Mustang
Top: 17"
MFG.: T.N.
Bottom: 8 1/2"
MFG.: Haji
Year: 1965

Ron Smith Collection

#124
Ford G T
Color: Red
Length: 10"
MFG.: Bandai, Japan
Power: Battery motor
Year: 1960's

#125
Ford Torino
Color: Red
Length: 16"
MFG.: S.T.
Power: Friction
Year: 1968

Ron Smith Collection

#126
Ford
Color: Green
Length: 12"
MFG.: Bandai, Japan
Power: Friction
Year: 1955

#127
Ford
Colors: Two tone blue, black and red
Length: 11 1/2"
MFG.: Haji
Power: Friction
Year: 1956

Rex Barrett Collection.

#128
Ford
Color: Yellow and white
Length: 13"
MFG.: Marusan
Power: Friction
Year: 1956

David Pressland Collection

#129
Ford
Color: Blue and white
Length: 13"
MFG.: Marusan
Power: Friction
Year: 1956

Ron Smith Collection

#130
Ford Sedan
Color: Red, white and black
Length: 12"
MFG.: Joustra, France
Power: Friction
Year: 1957

#131
Ford Convertible
Colors: Red and black, two tone green
Length: 12"
MFG.: Bandai
Power: Friction
Year: 1957

#132
Ford Wagon
Color: Blue and white
Length: 12"
MFG.: Bandai
Power: Friction
Year: 1957

#133
Ford Ranchero
Color: Black and red
Length: 12"
MFG.: Bandai
Power: Friction
Year: 1957

Jerry Byrne Collection

#134
Ford Ranchero
Color: Blue and white
Length: 12"
MFG.: Joustra, France
Power: Friction
Year: 1957

#135
Ford Thunderbird
Color: Orange
Length: 11"
MFG.: (T.N.)
Power: Battery (Electric lights)
Year: 1956

#136
Ford Thunderbird
Color: Blue and white
Length: 11"
MFG.: (T.N.)
Power: Battery (Electric lights)
Year: 1956

Note: Original box

#137
Ford Thunderbird
Color: Red
Length: 11"
MFG.: T.N., Japan
Power: Friction
Year: 1956

Note: Original box

#138
International Cement Mixer
Color: Red, orange and silver
Length: 19"
MFG.: (SSS)
Power: Pull-friction
Year: Early 50's

Fred Thompson Collection.
Note: Photo illustrating size of cement truck in comparison to Smith Miller Truck.

#138A
International Grain Hauler
Color: Red and Orange
Length: 23"
MFG.: (SSS)
Power: Pull-friction
Year: Early 50's

Fred Thompson Collection

#139
Lincoln Color: Two tone blue
Length: 12"
MFG.: Yonezawa
Power: Friction
Year: 1955

Rex Barrett Collection

#140
Lincoln Continental Mark II
Color: Black
Length: 12"
MFG.: Line Mar
Power: Friction or battery
Year: 1956

Ron Smith Collection

#141
Box Continental

Rex Barrett Collection

#142
Lincoln Continental and Cabin Cruiser
Overall length: 23"
MFG.: Bandai and Fleetline
Year: 1958

Note: Lincoln also sold by Bandai without boat. It came in a hardtop and convertible.

#143
Lincoln Mark III
Color: Blue and white
Length: 11"
MFG.: Bandai, Japan
Power: Friction motor
Year: 1958

#143A
Lincoln
Color: White and blue
Length: 12"
MFG.: Unknown
Power: Friction
Year: 1950's

David Pressland Collection

#144
Lincoln
Color: Red
Length: 10 1/2"
MFG.: Unknown, Japan
Power: Friction
Year: 1964

Ron Smith Collection

#145
Lincoln
Color: White and blue
Length: 16 1/2"
MFG.: Unknown
Power: Friction
Year: 1956

Ron Smith Collection

#146
Lincoln
Color: Black
Length: 11"
MFG.: (Y) Yonezawa, Japan
Power: Battery
Year: 1960

Note: Original box

#147
Lincoln
Color: Red
Length: 11"
MFG.: Cragstan
Power: Battery
Year: 1960

#148
Jaguar XK-150
Color: Blue and white
Length: 9 1/2"
MFG.: Bandai
Power: Friction
Year: 1960

#149
Jaguar XKE
Color: Blue
Length: 10 1/2"
MFG.: T.T.
Power: Friction
Year: 1960's

#150
Jaguar XKE
Color: Silver
Length: 10 1/2"
MFG.: Lendolet Auto
Power: Friction
Year: 1960's

#151
Jaguar XK-120
Color: Green
Length: 6 1/2"
MFG.: Alps
Power: Friction
Year: 1965

#152
Jaguar XK 140 - XK 150
Various colors
Length: 9 1/2"
MFG.: Bandai

David Pressland Collection

#153
Jaguar XK-E
Color: Red
Length: 10"
MFG.: Bandai, Japan
Power: Battery motor
Year: 1960's

#154
Isetta (3 wheels)
Colors: White and two tone green
Length: 6 1/2"
MFG.: Bandai, Japan
Power: Friction motor
Year: 1950's

#155
B M W 600 Isetta (4 wheels)
Color: Red and white
Length: 9''
MFG.: Bandai, Japan
Power: Friction motor
Year: 1950's

#156
Land Rover
Color: Red
Length: 7 1/2"
MFG.: Bandai
Power: Friction
Year: 1960

#157
Messerschmitt
Color: Red and white
Length: 8 1/2"
MFG.: Bandai
Power: Friction
Year: 1956

David Pressland Collection

#158
Mazda 360 Coupe
Color: Blue
Length: 7"
MFG.: Bandai
Power: Friction
Year: 1960

#159
Mazda Cosmo
Color: Yellow
Length: 15"
MFG.: (K.N.)
Power: Friction
Year: 1973

#160
Mazda Auto Tricycle
Color: Maroon and purple
Length: 8 1/2"
MFG.: Bandai
Power: Friction
Year: 1950's

Jerry Byrne Collection

#161
Lotus Elite
Color: Red and black
Length: 8 1/2"
MFG.: Bandai
Power: Friction
Year: 1950's

#162
Mercedes-Benz 300 SL
Color: White and red
Length: 11"
MFG.: (T.N.), Japan
Power: Battery
Year: 1950's

#163
Mercedes-Benz 300 SL
Color: Red
Length: 7"
MFG.: K S
Power: Battery (Electric lights)
Year: 1950's

#164
Mercedes-Benz 300 SL
Color: Red
Length: 9"
MFG.: Cragstan
Power: Battery
Year: 1950's

#165
Mercedes-Benz 300 SL
Color: Silver and black
Length: 8"
MFG.: Bandai
Power: Friction
Year: 1950's

#166
Mercedes-Benz 220S
Color: Black
Length: 12"
MFG.: (SSS)
Power: Battery
Year: 1962

Note: Benz came with electric headlights and without.

#167
Mercedes-Benz 250 S E
Color: Red
Length: 13"
MFG.: Ichiko
Power: Battery
Year: 1960's

#168
Mercedes-Benz 230 SL
Color: White and black
Length: 10"
MFG.: Alps
Power: Battery
Year: 1960's

#169
Mercedes-Benz 230 SL
Color: Red and black
Length: 10"
MFG.: Alps
Power: Battery
Year: 1960's

#170
Mercedes-Benz 300 SL
Color: Silver
Length: 8 1/2"
MFG.: Marusan
Power: Friction
Year: 1957-58

Jerry Byrne Collection

#171
Mercedes
Color: Black and white
Length: 12 1/2"
MFG.: Ichiko
Power: Friction
Year: 1960's

Jerry Byrne Collection

#172
Mercedes-Benz 600
Color: Red
Length: 10"
MFG.: Unknown, Japan
Power: Friction
Year: 1960's

Jerry Byrne Collection

112

#173
Mercedes-Benz 230 SL
Color: Tan and white
Length: 15"
MFG.: Modern Toys
Power: Battery
Year: 1960's

Jerry Byrne Collection

#174
Mercedes-Benz 230 SL
Color: Maroon and white
Length: 14 1/2"
MFG.: Yanoman
Power: Battery
Year: 1960's

Jerry Byrne Collection

#175
Mercedes-Benz 250 S
Color: White and red
Length: 14"
MFG.: Daiya
Power: Friction
Year: 1960's

Jerry Byrne Collection

#176
Mercedes-Benz
Color: Red
Length: 24''
MFG.: Ichiko
Power: Friction
Year: 1970

#177
Mercedes-Benz Taxi
Color: Black
Length: 10''
MFG.: Bandai
Power: Battery
Year: 1960's

#178
Mercedes-Benz Racer W 196
Color: Silver and red
Length: 10"
MFG.: Marusan, Japan
Power: Battery
Year: 1950's

#179
Mercedes-Benz Racer
Color: Red
Length: 9 1/2"
MFG.: Line Mar, Japan
Power: Friction
Year: 1950's

#180
Mercury Cougar
Color: Red
Length: 15"
MFG.: Asakusa Toys
Power: Friction
Year: 1967

#181
Mercury Cougar
Color: Red
Length: 10"
MFG.: Taiyo
Power: Battery
Year: 1967

#182
Mercury
Color: Grey and black
Length: 9 1/2"
MFG.: Rock Valley Toys, Japan
Power: Battery
Year: 1954

#183
Mercury
Color: Brown and white
Length: 11 1/2"
MFG.: Yonezawa
Power: Friction
Year: 1958

Ron Smith Collection

#184
Mercury
Color: Red and yellow
Length: 9 1/2"
MFG.: Alps
Power: Friction
Year: 1956

Ron Smith Collection

#185
MG TF
Color: Blue
Length: 8 1/2"
MFG.: Unknown, Japan
Power: Friction
Year: 1952

#186
MG TD
Color: Red and black
Length: 6 1/2"
MFG.: (SSS), Japan
Power: Friction
Year: 1954-55

#187
MG 1600 Mark II
Color: Red
Length: 8 1/2"
MFG.: Bandai
Power: Friction
Year: 1950's

Jerry Byrne Collection

118

#188
MG TF
Color: Green
Length: 8"
MFG.: (K O) Bandai
Power: Friction
Year: 1955

#189
MGA
Color: Red
Length: 10"
MFG.: (A.T.C.)
Power: Friction
Year: 1957

David Pressland Collection

#190
Nash
Color: Grey
Length: 8"
MFG.: MSK
Power: Battery
Year: 1950's

#191
Buick
Color: Red and white
Length: 8"
MFG.: Unknown
Power: Battery
Year: 1954

#192
Oldsmobile
Color: Blue and white
Length: 10 1/2"
MFG.: Unknown
Power: Friction
Year: 1956

#192A
1961 Asahi Toy Col., Ltd.
(Japan) Toy Catalog
A.T.C.

Anamorphose - Jacky Broutin Collection

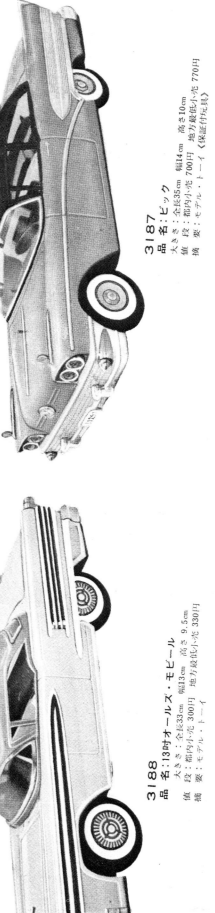

3463
品　名：14″ 赤十字ワゴン
大きさ：全長36cm　幅15cm　高さ 9.5cm
値　段：都内小売 300円　地方最低小売 330円
摘　要：動力玩具　後扉開閉出来ます。

3155
品　名：フォード
大きさ：全長20.5cm　幅 8.5cm　高さ 6.5cm
値　段：都内小売 100円　地方最低小売 110円
摘　要：モデル・トーイ

3187
品　名：ビック
大きさ：全長35cm　幅14cm　高さ10cm
値　段：都内小売 700円　地方最低小売 770円
摘　要：モデル・トーイ《保証付玩具》

3384
品　名：シボレー
大きさ：全長21.5cm　幅 9cm　高さ 6.5cm
値　段：都内小売 130円　地方最低小売 140円
摘　要：モデル・トーイ

3188
品　名：13吋オールズ・モビール
大きさ：全長33cm　幅13cm　高さ 9.5cm
値　段：都内小売 300円　地方最低小売 330円
摘　要：モデル・トーイ

#193
Oldsmobile
Color: Orange and white
Length: 16''
MFG.: (Y)
Power: Friction
Year: 1958

FRICTION OLDSMOBILE

#194
Oldsmobile
Color: Brown and white
Length: 12 1/2''
MFG.: Ichiko
Power: Friction
Year: 1959

Note: Also came in a police car.

#195
Oldsmobile
Color: Gold and black
Length: 12''
MFG.: (A.T.C.)
Power: Friction
Year: 1958

#196
Oldsmobile
Color: White
Length: 12"
MFG.: Yonezawa
Power: Friction
Year: 1961

Ron Smith Collection

#197
Olds Toronado
Color: Red
Length: 17 1/2"
MFG.: Ichiko
Power: Friction
Year: 1968

Ron Smith Collection

#198
Olds Toronado
Color: Gold
Length: 11"
MFG.: Bandai
Power: Battery
Year: 1966

#199
1961 Asahi Toy Co., Ltd. (A.T.C.)
(Japan) Toy Catalog

Anamorphose - Jacky Broutin
Collection

124

3552
品　名：ディフェンス・パトロールジープ
大きさ：全長28cm　幅12.7cm　高さ14cm
値　段：都内小売300円　地方最低小売330円
摘　要：サイレン作動力元具

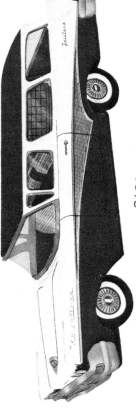

3186
品　名：14吋ステイション・ワゴン
大きさ：全長36cm　幅15cm　高さ9.5cm
値　段：都内小売300円　地方最低小売330円
摘　要：モデル・トーイ後部開閉出来ます

3558
品　名：トヨエース
大きさ：全長22.8cm　幅9.8cm　高さ10.2cm
値　段：都内小売200円　地方最低小売220円
摘　要：モデル・トーイ（運転台ダンプ・ホール）

3444
品　名：6吋スバル360
大きさ：全長15.5cm　幅7cm　高さ6.5cm
値　段：都内小売80円　地方最低小売90円
摘　要：モデル・トーイ

3534
品　名：シボレーステーションワゴン
大きさ：全長25.5cm　幅9.5cm　高さ7.5cm
値　段：都内小売140円　地方最低小売150円
摘　要：モデル・トーイ

#200
Opel
Color: Orange and green
Length: 11 1/2"
MFG.: (Y) Yonezawa
Power: Battery (Electric lights)
Year: 1950's

Note: Also came in a friction motor version.
(Red-silver)

#201
Opel
Color: White and red
Length: 11 1/2"
MFG.: (Y) Yonezawa
Power: Battery (Electric lights)
Year: 1950's

#202
Pontiac Firebird
Color: Red
Length: 15 1/2"
MFG.: Akasura
Year: 1967
Bottom-
Length: 10"
MFG.: Bandai
Year: 1967

Ron Smith Collection

#203
Pontiac Firebird
Color: Red
Length: 9 1/2"
MFG.: Bandai
Power: Battery
Year: 1967

#204
Packard Convertible
Packard Sedan
Length: 16"
MFG.: Alps
Power: Friction
Year: 1953

Bill Drake Collection

#205
Plymouth Hardtop
Color: Red and white
Length: 10 1/2''
MFG.: (A.T.C.)
Power: Friction
Year: 1959

Plymouth Convertible
Color: Red and white
Length: 10 1/2''
MFG.: (A.T.C.)
Power: Friction
Year: 1959

#207
Plymouth
Color: Red and white
Length: 12"
MFG.: Alps
Power: Battery
Year: 1956

#208
Plymouth T.V. Car
Color: Silver
MFG.: Ichiko
Power: Battery
Year: 1961

#209
Plymouth Fury
Color: White and red
Length: 11 1/2"
MFG.: (Y)
Year: 1957

Plymouth
Color: Black and red
Length: 8 1/2"
MFG.: Unknown
Year: 1956

Ron Smith Collection

#210
Plymouth Fury
Color: Black and red
Length: 10"
MFG.: Kusama
Power: Friction
Year: 1964

Jerry Byrne Collection

#211
Plymouth Ambulance
Length: 12"
MFG.: Bandai

Power: Friction
Year: 1961

Al Marwick Collection

#212
Plymouth
Color: Red and white
Length: 12"
MFG.: Ichiko

Power: Friction
Year: 1961

David Pressland Collection

#213
Porsche 911
Color: White
Length: 10"
MFG.: Bandai
Power: Battery
Year: 1960's

#214
Porsche
Color: Red
Length: 15"
MFG.: Unknown
Year: 1968

David Pressland Collection

#215
Porsche World News 911
Color: White and blue
Length: 9 1/2"
MFG.: T.R.S.
Power: Battery
Year: 1960's

#216
Porsche Rally Type 911
Color: White and blue
Length: 9 1/2"
MFG.: Alps
Power: Battery
Year: 1960's

#217
Porsche 924
Color: Red and white
Length: 8 1/2"
MFG.: Asahi
Power: Battery
Year: 1970's

#218
Studebaker
Color: Red
Length: 9"
MFG.: Japan
Year: 1953
Studebaker Avanti
Color: Blue
Length: 8"
MFG.: Bandai

Ron Smith Collection

#219
Studebaker
Color: Red
Length: 9"
MFG.: Unknown, Japan
Power: Friction
Year: 1953

Jerry Byrne Collection

#220
Toyota
Color: Red
Length: 16"
MFG.: Ichiko
Power: Friction
Year: 1967

Ron Smith Collection

#221
Toyota 2000 GT
Color: Red
Length: 15"
MFG.: A.T.C.
Power: Friction
Year: 1967

#222
Galant GTO Toyota
Color: Red
Length: 12 1/2"
MFG.: St. Nemoto
Power: Friction
Year: 1970's

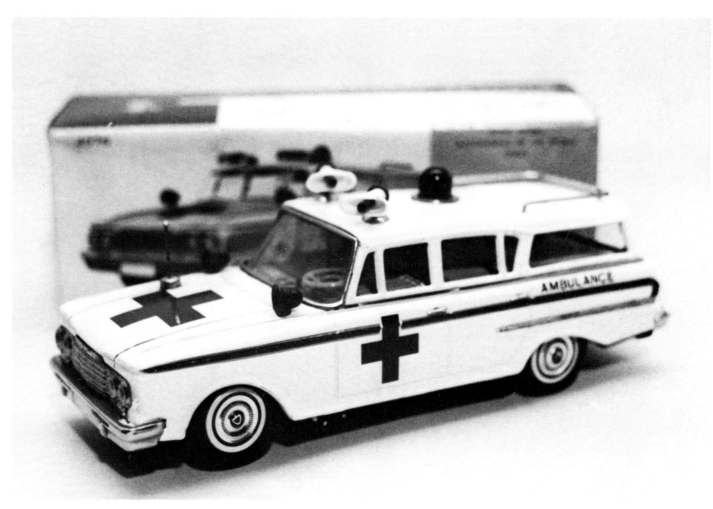

#223
Rambler Ambulance
Color: White
Length: 11"
MFG.: Bandai
Power: Friction
Year: 1962

Jerry Byrne Collection

#224
Rambler
Color: Red and white
Length: 10 1/2"
MFG.: N K Toys, Korea
Power: Friction
Year: 1961

#225
Austin
Color: Red and white
Length: 8"
MFG.: SK - Suda
Power: Friction
Year: 1958

#226
Renault 750
Length: 7"
MFG.: TM
Year: 1958
Renault 750
Length: 7 1/2"
MFG.: (Y)
Year: 1958

David Pressland Collection

#227
Rolls Royce
Length: 10 1/2''
MFG.: Unknown, Japan
Year: 1960

Al Marwick Collection

#228
Subaru 360
Color: Red
Length: 8"
MFG.: Bandai
Power: Friction
Year: 1959

#229
Volkswagen
Color: Red
Length: 8"
MFG.: Bandai, Japan
Power: Battery
Year: 1960's

#230
Volkswagen Convertible
Color: White
Length: 7 1/2"
MFG.: Bandai, Japan
Power: Battery
Year: 1960's

#231
Volkswagen
Color: Blue
Length: 8"
MFG.: Bandai
Power: Battery
Year: 1960's

#232
Volkswagen Bus
Color: Red and white
Length: 9 1/2"
MFG.: Bandai
Power: Battery
Year: 1960's

#233
Volkswagen Convertible
Color: Red
Length: 10 1/2"
MFG.: Taiyo
Power: Battery
Year: 1960's

#234
Volkswagen
Color: Blue
Length: 10 1/2"
MFG.: Bandai
Power: Battery
Year: 1960's

#235
Volkswagen
Color: Red
Length: 15''
MFG.: Bandai, Japan
Power: Battery
Year: 1960's

Note: Also came with a sun roof.

144

#236
Volkswagen Convertible
Color: Red or blue
Length: 9 1/2"
MFG.: (T.N.) Toy Nomura
Power: Friction
Year: 1950's

#237
Volkswagen Convertible
Color: White
Length: 12"
MFG.: (T.N.) Toy Nomura
Power: Battery
Year: 1960's

#238
Volkswagen Police Car
Color: White
Length: 9"
MFG.: Taiyo
Power: Battery
Year: 1970's

#239
Volkswagen
Color: Orange
Length: 10"
MFG.: Taiyo
Power: Battery
Year: 1970's

#240
Willy's Jeep FC-150
Color: Red or white
Length: 11"
MFG.: (T.N.) Toy Nomura
Power: Friction
Year: 1960

#241
Rambler, Trailer and Cabin Cruiser
Over length: 35"
MFG.: Bandai and Fleetline
Year: 1959

Note: The Rambler, Lincoln and Ferrari are the only three cars I've seen pulling these boats.

#242
Rambler Wagon and Shasta Trailer
Wagon-Green and white, Trailer-Yellow and white
Length: Wagon-11", Trailer-12"
MFG.: Bandai in conjunction with Fleet Line Boats, California
Year: 1959

Note: Shasta trailer also sold separately in its own box by Fleet Line, California

#243
Rambler Wagon and Cabin Cruiser
Overall length: 23"
MFG.: Bandai in conjunction with Fleet Line, California
Year: 1959

Note: The boats and electric motors were made in the United States. All cars are friction powered, boats have electric motors.

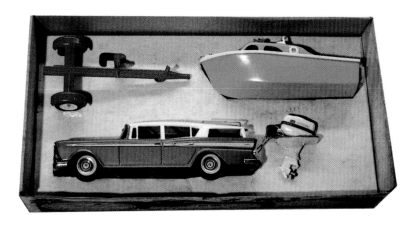

#244
Rolls-Royce Hardtop Convertible
Many colors available
Length: 12''
MFG.: Bandai, Japan
Power: Friction
Year: 1950's

#245
Rolls-Royce
Color: Blue, white, and black
Length: 12"
MFG.: Bandai, Japan
Power: Battery
Year: 1950's

Note: Rare with electric headlights.

#246
Champion's Racer
Color: Beige with red trim
Length: 18"
MFG.: Y
Power: Friction
Year: 1950's

Note: Champion's Racer also came with the words (Agajanian) instead of Champion's Racer which is much rarer.
(Agajanian, J.C. The Race Car Driver)
Original Box & Racer-C.W. Frey Collection.
Agajanian-C.W. Frey Collection.

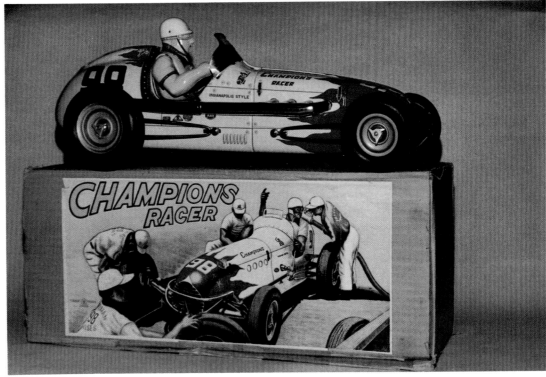

#247
Zuendapp Janus
Color: Red and white
Length: 8"
MFG.: Bandai
Power: Friction
Year: 1950's

Ron Hill Collection

#248
Ford Gyron
Color: Red and white
Length: 11"
MFG.: Ichida
Power: Battery
Year: 1960

#249
GM's Gas-Turbine-powered Firebird II
Color: Red
Length: 8 1/2"
MFG.: Unknown, Japan
Power: Friction
Year: 1956

Note: Featured in *Motor Trend*
Magazine 25¢ March 1956

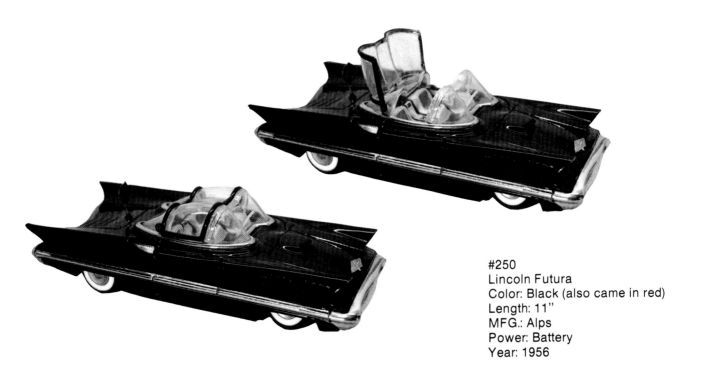

#250
Lincoln Futura
Color: Black (also came in red)
Length: 11"
MFG.: Alps
Power: Battery
Year: 1956

European Toy Companies

#251
Mercedes 190SL Kit
MFG.: Schuco
Year: 1960's
Schuco Toy Catalog 1966

FEDERWERK- UND

2010 „Magico", das Zauberauto mit vielen Tricks
Modell Alfa Romeo in Stahlausführung.
Startet und stoppt geheimnisvoll
• durch Berühren der Antenne
  oder Rücksitzablage
• durch scharfes Sprechen oder Blasen.
Steuerrad-Lenkung, zusätzliche Fernlenkung
durch beiliegende Fernlenkwelle und Handsteuerrad, Hindernissäulen.

3	510	23,5	×	—

2095 Fernlenk-Mercedes, verkehrsgerecht fernlenkbar
Modell Mercedes 190 SL in Stahlausführung.
Fernlenkung mit Rutschkupplung, Fernlenkwelle
und Handsteuerrad. Automatischer Stopphebel,
der das Federwerk nur dann ablaufen läßt, wenn
der Wagen auf die Lauffläche gestellt wird.
Säulen für Hindernisfahrt.

3	440	20,5	×	—

2097 Montage-Mercedes, der Autobaukasten mit echten Vorzügen
Modell Mercedes 190 SL in Stahlausführung.
Durch ausgereifte Konstruktion leicht zu montieren
• 46 Montageteile, nicht rostend
• kompletter Werkzeugsatz
• fertig montiertes Federwerk, vernickelt
• komplette Fernlenkeinrichtung, vernickelt
• nach Montage ein Fernlenkauto mit
  Präzisions-Steuerung.

3	715	44x29x5	×	⚡

3000 Fernlenk-Polizeiauto
Modell VW aus hochwertigem Zinkdruckguß.
Viele Spielmöglichkeiten durch die Fernlenkein-
richtung (Tisch- und Bodenspiele).
Federwerk mit Start- und Stopphebel und Ge-
schwindigkeits-Regulierung.
Stückpackung mit Fernlenkzubehör und bunten
Hindernissäulen.

3	235	18x10x5	×	⚡

#252
230 SL Mercedes
Color: Red
Length: 10"
MFG.: Schuco, Germany
Power: Battery
Year: 1960's

Ron Hill Collection
Schuco Toy Catalog 1966

schuco

5720 „Hydro-Car" Elektro-Fernlenkauto

Modell Mèrcedes Cabrio 220 S in Stahlausführung:

* sichtbar arbeitende Flüssigkeitskupplung (Bewegungsenergie eines in Umlauf gesetzten Flüssigkeitsstromes wird zur Kraftübertragung ausgenutzt)
* Lenkrad-Schaltung für Vorwärts- Rückwärtsfahrt und Stopp
* Fernlenkung mit beiliegender Fernlenkeinrichtung
* Steuerrad-Lenkung
* zu öffnender Kofferraumdeckel.

3	620	26	—	×

6080 Elektro-Konstruktions-Feuerwehr

Eine ausgereifte Konstruktion, die auf dem Weltmarkt unübertroffen ist.

* vollständig demontierbar und montierbar nach genauer Anleitung
* robuste Ausführung aus hochwertigem Zinkdruckguß und Stahlblech
* Original-Drehwindwerk mit vielen Details und 4-teiliger Ausfahrleiter (Länge: 85 cm)
* Kommandogerät für Elektro-Fernschaltung — Vorwärts- Rückwärtsfahrt und Stopp
* Hand-Steuerrad am Kommandogerät für Fernlenkung
* automatisches Aus- und Einfahren der Leiter über Kommandogerät, oder durch Handbetrieb
* viele technische Details wie Steigungswinkelmesser, Rücklaufsperre, Stützausleger, Getriebeschutzkasten, Handbremse, reichhaltiger Werkzeugsatz.

1	1820	25	—	×

5990 Verlängerungs-Kabel

für Trafo 5980 in Verbindung mit jeder Elektro-Fernlenkgarnitur

6084 Elektro „Lastomat" mit echter Ladebordwand

Modell MAN in Stahlausführung.

* Elektro-Antrieb durch Unterflurmotor, umschaltbar für Fahr- und Arbeitsbetrieb
* automatisch arbeitende Meiller-Ladebordwand aus Zinkdruckguß
* Rutschkupplung verhindert die Überlastung des leistungsfähigen Hebemechanismus
* selbsttätiges Schließen der Bordwand nach Ladevorgang
* Fernlenkung mit beiliegender Fernlenkeinrichtung

1	1210	36	—	×

6084 FG Elektro-Fernlenkgarnitur

ermöglicht Fernlenkung und Fernschaltung für Vorwärts- und Rückwärtsfahrt, sowie Fernbedienen der Ladebordwand.

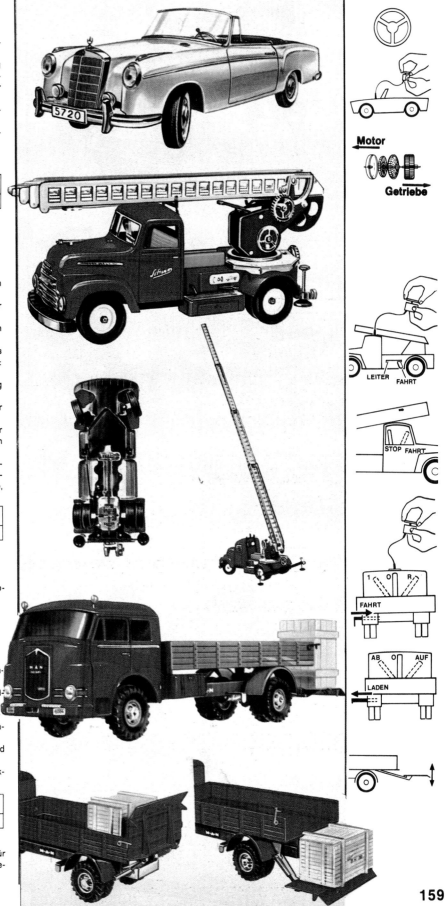

Motor

Getriebe

LEITER FAHRT

STOP FAHRT

1 O R
FAHRT

AB O AUF
LADEN

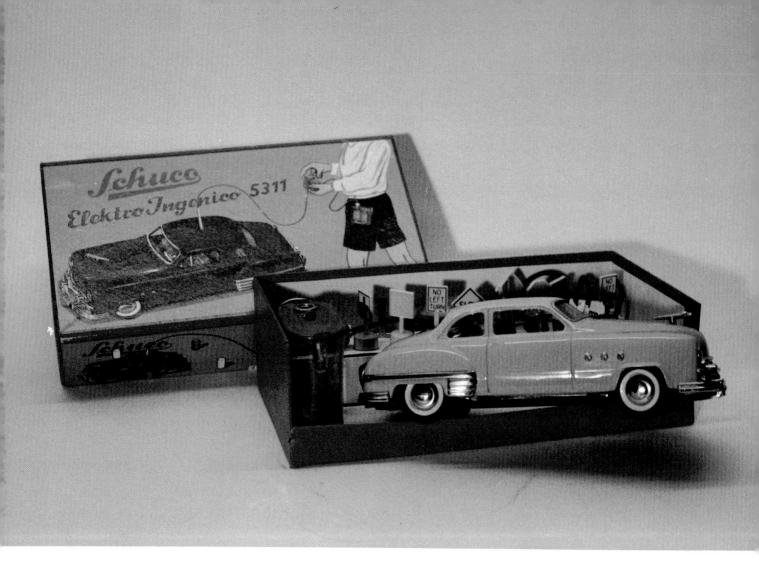

#253
Ingenico Electric Remote Control Car
Various Colors
Length: 8 3/4"
MFG.: Schuco, Germany
Power: Battery
Year: 1955

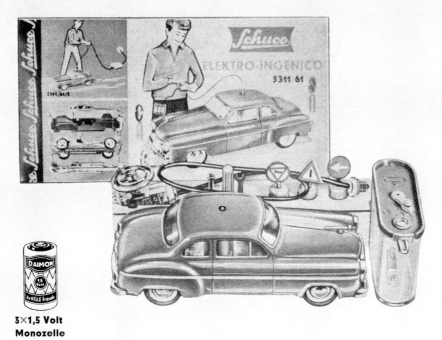

**3×1,5 Volt
Monozelle**

5311/61 Schuco-Ingenico-Elektro-Fern-lenkauto mit Fernschalteinrichtung für Vor- und Rückwärtsfahrt und Stop am Handschaltgerät. Fahrtgeschwindigkeits-regulierung am Batteriegehäuse für 3 große Stabzellen à 1,5 Volt; ganz montierbar. Betrieb kann auch über Schuco-Trafo 5980 erfolgen. Moderne Luxus-Limousine mit stromsparendem Hochleistungs-Doppelmagnet-Motor, Nickelbeschläge, Farben sortiert, 3 Verkehrszeichen und Werkzeug, farbiger Geschenkkarton.

Länge 22 cm, Gewicht 615 g

5311/61 S Schuco-Ingenico-Elektro-Fern-lenkauto mit Scheinwerferanlage. Funktion wie 5311/61 mit eingebauten Scheinwerfern, die am Batteriegehäuse auf- und abgeblendet werden können.

**3×1,5 Volt
Monozelle**

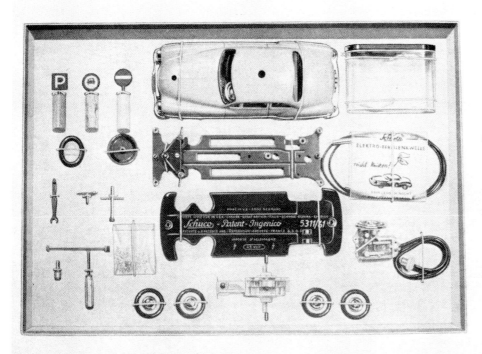

5311/61 MK Schuco-Ingenico-Elektro-Fernlenkauto in Montagekasten. Funktion wie 5311/61, Auto jedoch weitgehend auseinandergenommen in Montagekasten, mit Werkzeugen und Ersatzteilen, repräsentativer Geschenkkarton.

56,5×41×9,5 cm, Gewicht 1030 g

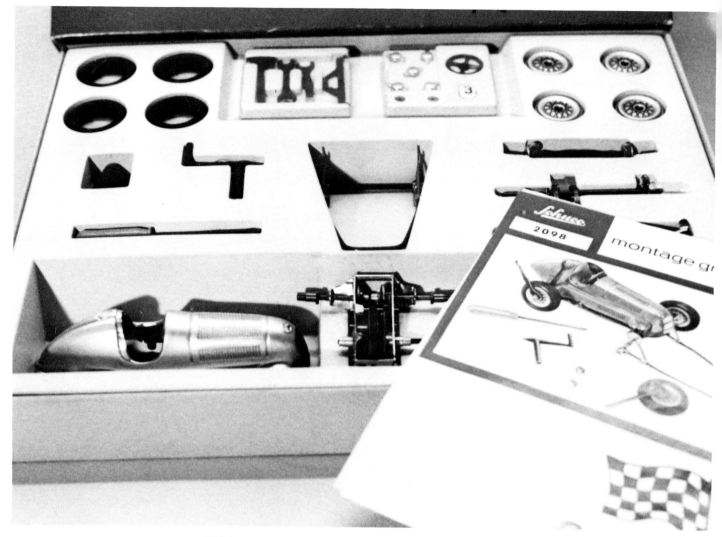

#254
Mercedes 1936 Grand-Prix Kit
MFG.: Schuco
Power: Clockwork
Year: 1962

Schuco Toy Catalog 1962-66
Pages 162-163

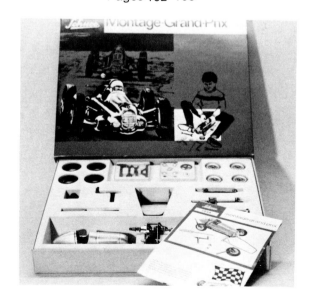

1050 Schuco-Studio-Auto, ein technisch interessantes Lenkauto mit sichtbarem Ausgleichsgetriebe (Differential) an der angetriebenen Hinterachse, Lenkradsteuerung, montierbaren Rädern und Reifen, automatische Leerlaufkupplung, Reibrad für schnellen Werkaufzug, der auch mittels Schlüssel vorgenommen werden kann, abnehmbares Steuerrad. Solide Metallausführung mit Nickelverzierungen, Werkzeugbeutel mit Schraubenschlüssel, Montiereisen und Ersatzmuttern sowie Aufziehkurbel, besonders robustes Federwerk, Farben sortiert, farbige Stückpackung.

Länge 14 cm, Gewicht 205 g

1060 Schuco-Studio-Montagekasten zum Zusammenbau des Studio-Rennwagens 1050, zusätzlich Wagenheber, Auto z. T. demontiert. 35 · 25 · 6 cm, Gewicht 555 g

1070 Schuco-Grand-Prix-Racer, modellgetreuer, besonders schnell- und langlaufender Ferrari-Rennwagen mit Lenkradsteuerung, montierbaren Rädern und Reifen, Handbremse, zwei Rückspiegeln, Windschutzscheibe zum Umklappen und Anstoßdämpfern. Besonders robustes Federwerk, Werkzeugbeutel mit Montiereisen und Schraubenschlüssel sowie Ersatzradkappen, Farben sortiert, farbige Stückpackung. Länge 16 cm, Gewicht 295 g

1080 Schuco-Rallyvox, Schwungradauto mit Hupo. Modernes Schwungradauto mit Lenkradsteuerung und einer Hupsignal-Einrichtung für Abgabe mehrerer hundert Signale bei einem Aufzug des Signalwerkes, Hupknopf am Lenkrad. Durch den einwandfrei laufenden Schwungradantrieb besonders für kleinere Kinder geeignet. Stabile Ausführung des modernen schnittigen Sportwagens in starkem Blech mit Nickelverzierungen, erstklassig lackiert, Farben sortiert, farbige Faltschachtel.

Länge 22 cm, Gewicht 355 g

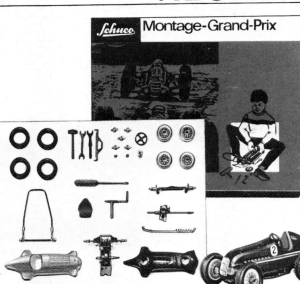

Montage-Grand-Prix

2098 Montage-Grand-Prix

Baukasten für ein technisch interessantes Lehr-
auto, Mercedes-Formel-Rennwagen 1936.
Ausgereifte Konstruktion — leicht zu montieren
* 26 nicht rostende Montage-Teile
* Rennsport-Wagenheber und verschiedenes
  Werkzeug
* fertig montiertes Federwerk, vernickelt
Das montierte Auto bietet:
* Schlüssel- oder Reibradschnellaufzug
* sichtbar arbeitendes Differential (Aus-
  gleichsgetriebe)
* Steuerrad-Lenkung
* automatische Leerlaufkupplung
* Größe des montierten Autos: 13,5 cm
* Stahlausführung

	9			
2	710	37 x 29 x 4	x	-

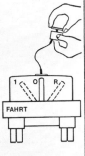

5306 Elektro-Fernlenk-LKW „MAN"

Ein Fernlenk-LKW, der in seiner robusten und
soliden Ausführung so recht zum Spiel geeignet
ist:
* Fernlenkung mit beiliegender Fernlenkwelle und Handsteuerrad
* Schalthebel für Vor- und Rückwärtsfahrt
* zu öffnende Rückbordwand
* 6fach gummibereift
* Stahlausführung.

	9			
2	1090	36	-	x

5307 Elektro-Fernlenkauto
„Mercedes 230 SL"

Ein sehr wirkungsvoll ausgestattetes, modell-
getreues Auto, mit einer robusten Stahl-
Karosserie.
* mit Zündschlüssel! Dadurch echtes Anlassen und Abschalten des leistungsfähigen
  Elektro-Motors
* Fernlenkung mit beiliegender Fernlenkwelle und Handsteuerrad
* zu öffnender Kofferraumdeckel
* Steuerradlenkung.

	9			
2	655	26,5	-	x

600 „Spiralograph" — das Wunder-
zeichengerät

Ein lehrreiches, unterhaltsames Beschäftigungs-
spiel für alle Altersstufen.
* in kürzester Zeit können die wunder-
  barsten Spiral-Ornamente auf das Papier
  gezaubert werden
* unendliche Kombinationsmöglichkeiten
  durch die Wahl verschiedener Farbstifte
  und Führungsringe
* für den künstlerisch arbeitenden „Desig-
  ner"
* Zeichenpapier liegt bei
* Vorlageheft mit Anregungen
* handelsübliche Farbminen können überall
  nachgekauft werden.
Inhalt: 1 Zeichenscheibe mit 13 Buchsen, 1 Griff,
        3 Führungsringe, 4 Spezialhalter mit ver-
        schiedenfarbigen Kugelschreiberminen,
        1 Vorlagenbuch, Zeichenpapier.

spiralograph

	9			
2	435	42 x 29 x 4	-	-

#255
Packard Hawk
Length: 10 3/4"
MFG.: Schuco
Year: 1957

Bill Drake Collection

Radioauto mit Schallverstärkung und Fahr-Elektroantrieb!

2 × 1,5 Volt
Babyzellen

5710 Schuco-Elektro-Radio-Car, modernes Stromlinien-Auto mit am Armaturenbrett ein- und abschaltbarem eingebautem 18-stimmigem Schweizer Markenmusikwerk. Durch die neue Schallverstärkungsanlage wird ein besonders reiner Ton und eine bisher noch nicht erzielte Lautstärke erreicht. Der stabile und unempfindliche Elektromotor wird mit zwei einfach einzulegenden 1,5-Volt-Babyzellen betrieben. Der Wagen kann durch einen Drehknopf am Armaturenbrett gestartet und gestoppt werden. Antenne zum Herausziehen, Lenkradsteuerung, Farben sortiert, farbige Faltschachtel. Länge 27,5 cm, Gewicht 560 g.

Schuco toy Catalog 1962

Ein Wagen für den fortschrittlichen kleinen Autofahrer!

5700 Schuco-Elektro-Synchromatic, Modell Packard

2 × 1,5 Volt Babyzellen

mit 7-facher, vollautomatischer Schaltung für verschiedene Fahrvorgänge mit Lichtsignal, Drucktasten-Gangschaltung, Fernlenkung, Auflademöglichkeit der Trockenbatterien durch Trafo.

Nach Betätigung des Schalters beginnt der Motor des Autos automatisch im Stand zu laufen. Der Automat schaltet dann nach Aufleuchten der roten Lampe am Armaturenbrett den 1. Gang ein und das Auto setzt sich in Bewegung. Nach kurzer Fahrt erfolgt nach jeweiligem kurzem Aufleuchten der Signallampe Umschaltung auf Schnellgang, dann zurück auf denn ersten Gang, dann auf Stop, dann auf Rückwärtsgang und wieder auf Stop. Der Schaltvorgang wiederholt sich automatisch beliebig oft. Außerdem läßt sich das Auto vom Armaturenbrett aus mit modernster Drucktasten-Gangschaltung beliebig von Hand auf den Langsam-, Schnell- oder Rückwärtsgang schalten bzw. stoppen.

Antrieb des Elektroautos erfolgt mittels 2 × 1,5-Volt-Babyzellen. Die normale Betriebsdauer der Batterien kann mit der bekannten Schuco-Tanksäule 5506 und des Schuco-Trafos 5980 bis zu 60 Stunden verlängert werden.

Das Auto kann mit beiligender Fernlenkwelle und Lenkrad ferngelenkt werden.

Ausführung der Metallkarosserie: modellgetreu, mehrfarbig handlackiert, mit reicher Nickelverzierung, Lenkradsteuerung, Fernlenkung, robuster Elektro-Motor, Farben sortiert, farbige Stückpackung. Länge 28 cm, Gewicht 850 g.

#256
Mercedes 190 SL
Length: 8 5/8"
MFG.: Schuco
Power: Clockwork
Year: 1962

#257
Mercedes 230 SL
Length: 8 1/2"
MFG.: Schuco
Power: Battery
Year: 1965

#258
Mercedes 190 SL
Length: 8 5/8"
MFG.: Schuco
Power: Clockwork
Year: 1962

Schuco Toy Catalog 1966

5503 Elektro „Phaenomenal" Fernlenkauto

Modell Mercedes 190 SL, in Stahlausführung.

* Lenkradschaltung für Vorwärts-, Rückwärtsfahrt und Stopp
* Fernlenkung mit beiliegender Fernlenkeinrichtung
* Steuerrad-Lenkung
* Motorhaube und Kofferraumdeckel sind zu öffnen
* elektrisch „auftankbar" (Spieldauer mit 1 Batterie wird dadurch wesentlich verlängert) erforderliches Zubehör:
  Nr. 5506 Elektro-Tanksäule
  Nr. 5980 Vielzweck-Transformator
  (4,5 Volt =, Netzspannung angeben!)

🔋	⚖️9	↔	T	⚡
2	520	21	—	×

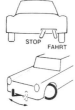

5509 Elektro „Razzia-Car", Polizeistreifenwagen mit Blaulicht

Modell Mercedes 190 SL, in Stahlausführung. Echte Spielfunktion mit originalgetreuem Blaulichtblinker, zwei Polizeifiguren als Besatzung. Motorhaube kann geöffnet werden. Die Vorderräder sind zur Lenkung einstellbar.

🔋	⚖️9	↔	T	⚡
2	450	21	—	×

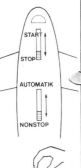

5600 Elektro „Radiant" Verkehrsflugzeug

Modell Vickers Viscount in Stahlausführung. Führt Startvorgang eines Flugzeuges in 8 Stufen aus.

* einzelner Anlauf der 4 Motoren
* Umschalten der Motoren auf Hochtouren
* Anrollen der Maschine zur Fahrt
* Anhalten des Flugzeuges
* Abschalten der Motoren nacheinander
* Hebel für Automatik und „Nonstop"-Betrieb
* Bugrad lenkbar, mit beiliegender Fernlenkeinrichtung
* elektrisch „auftankbar" wie Artikel 5503 (erforderlich: Trafo 5980, Tanksäule 5506 oder Tankwagen 5601)

Lieferbar als „LUFTHANSA", „PAA", „SWISSAIR", „KLM", „BOAC", „SABENA".

🔋	⚖️9	↔	T	⚡
2	1670	48	—	×

5700 Elektro „Synchromatic" vollautomatisches Schaltauto

Luxus-Limousine, in Stahlausführung.

* vollautomatische Stufenschaltung: Vorwärts: langsam, schnell, langsam — stopp — rückwärts — stopp.
* jeder automatische Schaltvorgang wird durch Lichtzeichen am Armaturenbrett angezeigt
* wahlweise Drucktasten-Gangschaltung für die gleichen Funktionen.
* Fernlenkung mit beiliegender Fernlenkeinrichtung
* Steuerrad-Lenkung
* elektrisch „auftankbar" wie Artikel 5503.

🔋	⚖️9	↔	T	⚡
2	850	26,5	—	×

#259
Mercedes 220 S
Length: 10''
MFG.: Schuco
Year: 1962

#260
Mercedes 230 SL
Length: 10 1/2''
MFG.: Schuco
Year: 1960's

Schuco Toy Catalog 1966

ELEKTRO-FERNLENKAUTOS

schuco

4003 „Combinato"

Lehrauto mit Lenkrad-Reihenschaltung für 3 Vorwärtsgänge, Rückwärtsgang und Leerlauf. Tachometer zeigt eingeschaltete Gänge und vergleichbare Geschwindigkeiten an. Hupsignalwerk für mehrere 100 Signale bei einem Aufzug. Steuerrad-Lenkung, Handbremse. Stahlausführung.

🔋	⚖️9	↔	T	⚡
3	335	19	×	—

4004 „Examico II"

Fahrschulauto mit Knüppelschaltung, 4 Vorwärtsgänge, Rückwärtsgang und Leerlauf (H-Schaltung). Steuerrad-Lenkung. Handbremse, Stahlausführung.

🔋	⚖️9	↔	T	⚡
3	285	19	×	—

5308 Elektro „Controll-Car"
Fernlenkauto mit Licht

Modell Mercedes 220 S Cabrio, in Stahlausführung.
* Kommandogerät für Elektro-Fernschaltung Vorwärts-, Rückwärtsfahrt und Stopp
* Handsteuerrad am Kommandogerät für Fernlenkung
* Steuerrad-Lenkung
* Scheinwerfer-Beleuchtung
* Batteriegehäuse für 2 x 1,5 Volt Monozellen
* Säulen für Geschicklichkeitsfahrten, Werkzeug.

🔋	⚖️9	↔	T	⚡
2	640	26	—	×

5340/1 Elektro „Alarm-Car"
Fernlenkauto mit Sirene

Modell Opel Admiral, in Stahlausführung.
* abstellbare Elektro-Zweiton-Sirene
* Blaulichtblinker
* Vierfunktionsschaltung: Fahrt, Fahrt mit Blaulicht, Fahrt mit Blaulicht und Sirene, Stopp.
* Fernlenkung mit beiliegender Fernlenkeinrichtung.

🔋	⚖️9	↔	T	⚡
2	515	21	—	×

5340 FG Elektro-Fernlenk-Garnitur
für 5340/1
Diese Zusatzgarnitur ermöglicht Fernschaltung für Vorwärts-, Rückwärtsfahrt und Stopp, sowie Fernlenkung (3 Volt).

Der Traumwagen jedes Kindes!

5500 „Real"-Elektro-Fernlenkauto mit Knüppelschaltung

Mercedes 230 SL in Stahlausführung.
* sichtbar arbeitendes, vollsynchronisiertes Getriebe. 4 Vorwärtsgänge, Rückwärtsgang und Leerlauf
* Original-Knüppelschaltung
* Zündschlüssel zum echten Anlassen und Abschalten des Motors
* Motorhaube und Kofferraumdeckel sind zu öffnen
* Fernlenkung mit beiliegender Fernlenkeinrichtung
* Steuerrad-Lenkung

🔋	⚖️9	↔	T	⚡
2	755	26,5	—	×

6080 FG Elektro-Fernlenk-Garnitur für 5500
wie 5340/1 jedoch für 4,5 Volt

#261
Old Timer Series
Length: 8''
MFG.: Schuco
Year: 1962

Schuco Old Timer Catalog, Germany

Oldtimer-Modelle Nr. 1225-1229
Einmalige Spielmöglichkeiten durch:
* hörbar laufenden Motor, robustes
  Federwerk
* Rüttelbewegung im Stand und während
  der Fahrt
* Kulissenschaltung
* Steuerrad-Lenkung
* Freilauf
* Bremse

modellgetreue Details, Gummibereifung, Stahlausführung. Zusätzliche Funktionen siehe Ein-
zelbeschreibung.

1225 Oldtimer „Mercer" Typ 35 J,
Baujahr 1913
Funktionen und Ausführung wie oben.

🔋	⬛9	⬌	T	⚡
3	550	18,5	×	–

1227 Oldtimer „Ford Coupe T",
Baujahr 1917
Funktionen und Ausführung wie oben.

🔋	⬛9	⬌	T	⚡
3	575	17,5	×	–

1228 Oldtimer „Opel Doktorwagen",
Baujahr 1909
Zusätzliche Spielmöglichkeit:
automatisches Klappverdeck, Öffnen und Schließen mit Motorkraft durch Knopfdruck, Vorgang
kann mehrmals wiederholt werden.
Sonstige Funktion und Ausführung wie oben.

🔋	⬛9	⬌	T	⚡
3	570	18,5	×	–

1229 Oldtimer „Mercedes Simplex"
Tourenwagen, Baujahr 1902
Zusätzliche Spielmöglichkeit:
mit der Anlaßkurbel wird der Federmotor echt
„angeworfen", Vorgang kann mehrmals wiederholt werden. Klappbares Verdeck.
Sonstige Funktion und Ausführung wie oben.

🔋	⬛9	⬌	T	⚡
3	610	20,5	×	–

4014 Oldtimer „Musical Car",
Ford Coupe T, Baujahr 1917
Hochwertiges 18-stimmiges Musikwerk, Steuerrad-Lenkung, Freilauf, Bremse, Stahlausführung,
goldfarbig Ohne Laufwerk.

🔋	⬛9	⬌	T	⚡
2	560	17,5	Musikwerk	–

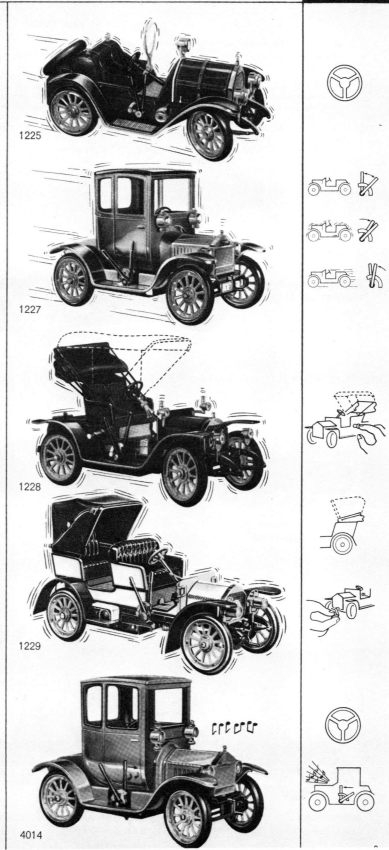

1225

1227

1228

1229

4014

#262
Alfa Romeo with driver
Length: 9 1/2"
MFG.: Schuco
Year: 1960's

#263
Alfa Romeo
Length: 9 1/2"
MFG.: Schuco
Year: 1960's

Schuco Toy Catalog 1962

Erstmals Flüssigkeitskupplung in einem Spielzeugauto!

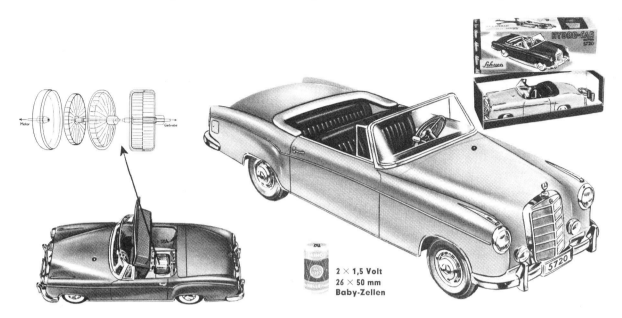

5720 Schuco-Hydro-Car, Mercedes 220 S, mit Original Flüssigkeitskupplung, bei der die Bewegungsenergie eines in Umlauf gesetzten Flüssigkeitsstromes zur Kraftübertragung ausgenutzt wird. Die Flüssigkeitskupplung zeichnet sich beim Spielzeugauto genau wie in der Großtechnik durch besonders weiche Arbeitsweise und sehr geringen Verschleiß aus. Der Elektromotor wird geschont, da die Kupplung jeden Widerstand, der sich auf den Elektromotor auswirken könnte, automatisch auffängt, so läuft der Motor z. B. bei Anstoß automatisch im Leerlauf weiter. Ein hochzuklappender Sitz ermöglicht ein genaues Studium der Arbeitsweise der Kupplung. Lenkradschaltung für Vor- und Rückwärtsfahrt und Stop Mit einer beiliegenden Fernlenkwelle ist das Auto fernlenkbar, kann aber auch vom Steuerrad aus beliebig gesteuert werden. Der leistungsfähige Elektromotor wird durch zwei in den Gepäckraum einfach einzulegende 1,5-Volt-Babyzellen betrieben, Farben sortiert,. Ausführung mit Chromverzierungen. Farbige Faltschachtel. Länge 25,8 cm, Gewicht 620 g.

Die denkende Autofahrerin lenkt, schaltet, fährt und schaut!

5735   Schuco-Texi

Auf **Automatic** gestellt, lenkt die Fahrerin, wie ein großer Autofahrer, das Steuer sichtbar mit den Händen und Armen und bewegt dabei den Kopf in die eingeschlagene Fahrtrichtung, nach rechts, links, geradeaus und rückwärts. Kurz vor der Rückwärtsfahrt schaltet die Figur mit der rechten Hand den Lenkradschalthebel um, dreht den Oberkörper und schaut dabei nach rückwärts. Das Auto führt automatisch folgende Fahrmanöver durch: Eine Acht vorwärts, stop, einen Kreis rückwärts, stop usw. Texi ist auch **fernlenkbar** für Vorwärtsfahrt, wobei die Figur mit den Händen und Armen synchron zu den Radeinschlägen das Steuer lenkt und mit dem Kopf jeweils in die eingeschlagene Fahrtrichtung schaut.

Wird das Auto aufgezogen oder in aufgezogenem Zustand von der Fahrtfläche hochgenommen, so stoppt es automatisch, bis es wieder auf die Fahrfläche aufgesetzt wird.

Ausstattung mit sehr stabilem, langlaufendem Qualitätsfederwerk, handlackiert, Chrombeschläge, Figur farbig gekleidet, kompl. Fernlenkeinrichtung mit Handsteuerrad und Fernlenkwelle, 2 Aufstellsäulen für Geschicklichkeitsspiele, Farben sortiert. Farbiger Karton. Länge 25 cm, Gewicht 695 g.

#264
Renault Frigate
Length: 12"
MFG.: CIJ, France
Power: Clockwork

#265
Renault
Length: 12"
MFG.: CIJ, France
Power: Clockwork

#266
Panhard
Length: 10"
MFG.: CIJ, France
Power: Clockwork

#267
Cadillac
Color: Yellow and white
Length: 12''
MFG.: Gama, Germany
Power: Friction
Year: 1954

#268
Cadillac Convertible
Color: Blue
Length: 12''
MFG.: Gama, Germany
Power: Friction
Year: 1954

#269
Opel
Color: Yellow and white
Length: 10"
MFG.: Gama, Germany
Power: Friction
Year: 1950's

#270
1954 Gama Toy Catalog

Anamorphose - Jacky Broutin Collection

Note: This toy catalog shows the Gama 1954 Cadillac.

178

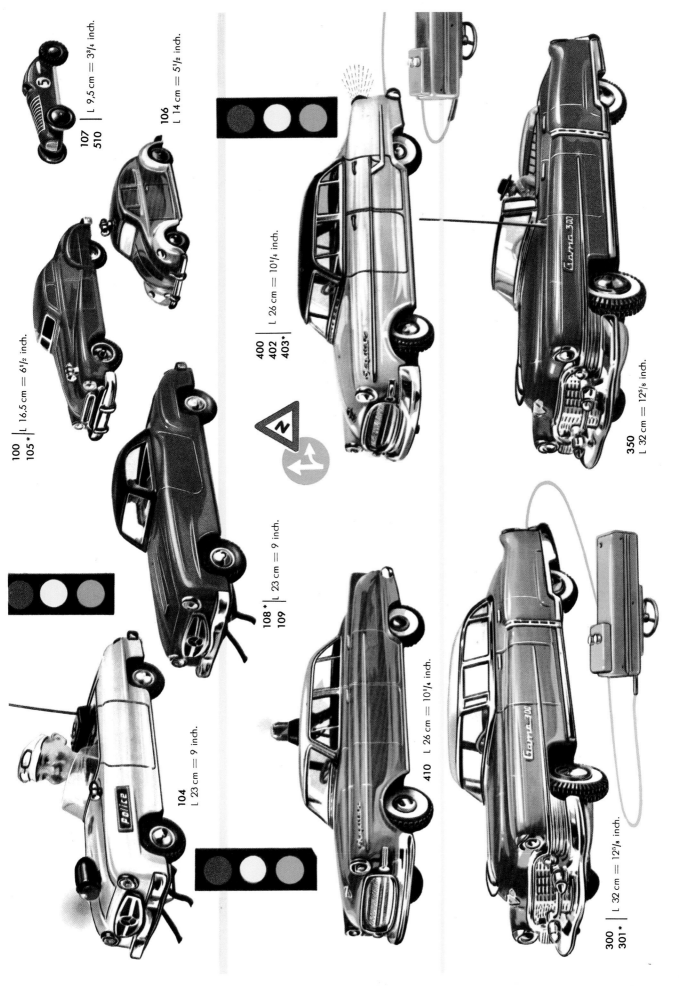

107
510 | L 9,5 cm = 3³/₄ inch.

106 | L 14 cm = 5¹/₂ inch.

100
105 * | L 16,5 cm = 6¹/₂ inch.

400
402
403* | L 26 cm = 10¹/₄ inch.

350 | L 32 cm = 12⁵/₈ inch.

108 *
109 | L 23 cm = 9 inch.

104 | L 23 cm = 9 inch.

410 | L 26 cm = 10¹/₄ inch.

300
301* | L 32 cm = 12⁵/₈ inch.

#271
Truck
Length: 15''
MFG.: Gama, Germany
Power: Clockwork
Year: 1950's

#272
1954 Gama Toy Catalog

Anamorphose - Jacky Broutin Collection

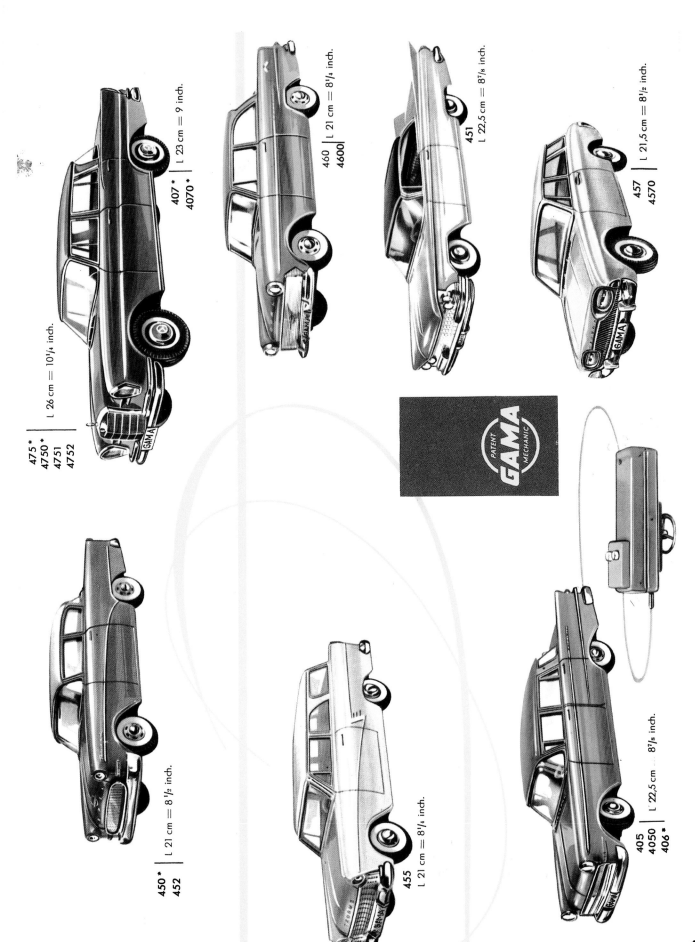

475*
4750*
4751
4752

L 26 cm = 10¹/₄ inch.

407*
4070*

L 23 cm = 9 inch.

460
4600

L 21 cm = 8¹/₄ inch.

451

L 22,5 cm = 8⁷/₈ inch.

457
4570

L 21,5 cm = 8¹/₂ inch.

450*
452

L 21 cm = 8¹/₂ inch.

455

L 21 cm = 8¹/₄ inch.

405
4050
406*

L 22,5 cm = 8⁷/₈ inch.

GAMA PATENT MECHANIC

#273
Volkswagen Bus
Length: 9"
MFG.: Tipp & Co.
Power: Battery (Electric lights)
Year: 1950's

Note: Original box

#274
Mercedes
MFG.: Tipp and Co., Germany

Dr. Reinhard Kunz Collection

#275
Dream Car
MFG.: Tipp and Co., Germany

Dr. Reinhard Kunz Collection

#276
Arnold Gas Station
Dimensions: 7 x 14 x 5
Year: 1950's

#277
Hot Rod
Length: 10"
MFG.: Arnold
Power: Spring Action
Year: 1950's

#278
1950's Chrysler
Length: 11"
MFG.: Gunthermann
Power: Friction
Year: 1950's

#279
49 Ford
Length: 11"
MFG.: SG Gunthermann
Power: Clockwork

#280
Wagon (resembles Buick wagon)
Color: Mint green
Length: 11"
MFG.: JAJ, Portugal
Power: Friction
Year: 1950's

#281
1958 Chrysler
Length: 13"
MFG.: Unknown—West Germany
Power: Battery

Note: Alps of Japan made a
14" Chrysler in 1957 (very
rare)

Jack Herbert Collection.

#282
Alfa Romeo
Length: 14"
MFG.: Ventura, Italy
Power: Battery
Year: 1954

#283
Mercedes Benz
Length: 9 1/2"
MFG.: (JNF) Johann Neuhieal, Germany
Power: Clockwork and electric
Year: 1950's

#284
Mercedes Benz
Length: 9 1/2"
MFG.: (JNF) Johann Neuhieal, Germany
Power: Clockwork
Year: 1950's

#285
Porsche Prototype
Color: Silver
Length: 8"
MFG.: JNF, Germany
Power: Clockwork
Year: 1950's

Jerry Byrne Collection

#286
Car
Length: 7 1/2"
MFG.: JNF - Johann Neuhieal
Power: Clockwork

#287
Cabriolet
Color: Red
Length: 10"
MFG.: Arnold
Power: Clockwork
Year: 1950's

#288
Cabriolet
Color: Blue
Length: 10"
MFG.: Arnold
Power: Clockwork
Year: 1955

#289
1952 Packard
Length: 10"
MFG.: Arnold, West Germany
Power: Spring action
Year: 1950's

#290
Mercedes
Length: 9 1/2"
MFG.: Distler
Power: Clockwork
Year: 1950's

#291
Porsche Speedster Police Car
Color: White
Length: 10 1/2"
MFG.: Distler, Germany
Power: Battery operated
Year: 1950's

Note: Police car is much harder to find in the United
States than the regular Distler Porsche.

#292
Porsche Speedster
Colors: Grey, blue, and red
Length: 10 1/2"
MFG.: Distler, Germany
Power: Battery operated
Year: 1950's

Note: Removable key in dash-board often is missing.

#293
Jaguar XK 120
Color: Red
Length: 8 1/2"
MFG.: Distler
Power: Friction
Year: 1950's

Jerry Byrne Collection

#294
Renault
Length: 12"
MFG.: Joustra, France
Power: Battery
Year: 1960's

#295
Peugeot
Length: 12"
MFG.: Joustra, France
Power: Battery
Year: 1960's

#296
Peugeot Ambulance
Length: 12"
MFG.: Joustra, France
Power: Battery
Year: 1960's

Rarity Guide

In grading these cars it is imperative to remember that a very rare car is worth considerably less if in poor condition. Condition is a key factor in collecting any kind of toy, so always let that be your primary consideration.

We will use a scale from one to five to determine the rarity and desirability of the toy cars pictured in this book.

Dale Kelley

1/ The rarest and most desired of all post war toy cars (very few known in collections)
2/ Very scarce and desirable (hard to find, but not impossible)
3/ Very desirable and getting scarcer (prices going up fast in this area, buy one now)
4/ Desirable but common (always worth picking up an extra one for trading)
5/ Very common (most collectors have one or more)

Note: There are no captions #13, 14 and 15.

LIBRARY

NATURAL HISTORY MUSEUM
LOS ANGELES COUNTY